Zen Contemplation
for Christians

Zen Contemplation
for Christians

Elaine MacInnes

SHEED & WARD

Lanham, Chicago, New York, Toronto, and Oxford

Published by Sheed & Ward
An Imprint of Rowman & Littlefield Publishers, Inc.

A Member of the Rowman & Littlefield Publishing Group
4501 Forbes Boulevard, Suite 200
Lanham, MD 20706

PO Box 317
Oxford
OX2 9RU, UK

Distributed by National Book Network

Library of Congress Cataloging-in-Publication Data

MacInnes, Elaine.
    Zen contemplation for Christians / Elaine MacInnes.
        p. cm.
    Originally published: Ottawa, Canada, c.2001
    Includes bibliographical references (p.).
    ISBN 1-58051-133-3 (pbk. : alk. Paper)
    1. Zen Meditations. 2. Christianity and other religions—Buddhism.
3. Buddhism—Relations—Christianity. I. Title

    BQ9269.4.C5M33 2003
    248.3´4—dc21   2003042485

Printed in the United States of America.

⊗™ The paper used in this publication meets the minimum
requirements of American National Standard for Information
Sciences—Permanence of Paper for Printed Library Materials,
ANSI/NISO Z39.48-1992.

• Dedication

To all my teachers in creation's family
the myriad conveyers of wisdom

Contents

Acknowledgments

I would like to acknowledge my gratitude to Michael O'Hearn and my editor, Kevin Burns, both at Novalis in Ottawa.

To Maria Delia Zamora of Toronto who assembled the cover artwork, and who provided computer expertise throughout.

To Sandy Chubb of Oxford, who read the entire manuscript with red pencil in hand.

To Sheena Davis of Wroxton, Oxfordshire, whose lovely painting seems so appropriate.

Although they remain in my heart, I cannot name all the people who made this story possible. To those named and unnamed in the book, I gratefully acknowledge a long life of connection and reciprocity.

And my eternal gratitude to the consummate SOURCE of life, light, and love.

Author's Note

In Japanese, the word coined for one's 77th birthday year is *biju*, replete with joy and happiness. When asked to write this book, which was to be in great measure autobiographical, I found many occasions to reflect on a long lifetime overflowing with gold. As a missioner I was gradually returning to Canada after an absence of about 40 years, and with much of the Western world, celebrating the turn of the third millennium in our recorded history. There was much to reminisce about, adventures in discoveries, places and people. My thoughts and subsequent notes came out in spurts, and are in no way chronological.

When a symphony orchestra comes on the stage to prepare for a concert, the oboe player rises and sounds the note A. The first violinist picks it up, tunes his or her violin, keeps sounding that intonation for the rest of the orchestra, and only after all that is accomplished will the conductor come out and the principal work begin. Chapter 1 is my oboe note.

Chapters 2 to 9 are a series of reminiscences, interspersed with some of the teachings and experiences of Oriental origins I received, because my weekly mailbag is stuffed with questions about that aspect of my life. I could have ended there, but my musical career has educated me to the value of an encore, which is a miniature in intimate light tones, and so I added chapter 10.

To old friends and new, I offer these pages in grateful celebration.

Elaine MacInnes
Toronto, Ontario
July 2001

Preface

Those of us who live in Japan know well that the great challenge facing Christianity in Asia is inculturation. We see that the Gospel of Jesus Christ must be preached to all nations in a language the people will understand; it must be preached in harmony with the rich culture that has been created in Asia by men and women of genius. And already we have a tiny glimpse of an Asian Christianity that speaks not only to the countries of Asia, but also to Europe and America and Africa. Can we not hope that the twenty-first century will see a Christianity that is truly global while retaining the characteristics of each culture?

In this task of building a new Christianity, Sister Elaine plays an important role. Having lived in Japan for several decades she has steeped herself in the culture of Asia. She has practiced Zen under the most outstanding teachers, who have recognized the depths of her enlightenment and wisdom. At the same time she has deepened her Christian commitment to Jesus Christ and the Gospel. While showing remarkable insight into the Zen *satori* and the Hindu *advaita* she continues to see more deeply into the riches of the New Testament. Throughout her writing, as throughout her life, echo the words of St. Paul: "I live, now not I; but Christ lives in me." She quotes from St. John of the Cross: "Love is my only destiny." She finds nourishment in the thirteenth-century mystic Meister Eckhart and in a classical book of the Jesuit Paul de Jaegher, *One with Jesus*. And in uniting East and West she evinces none of the anguish that characterizes some others who have written on this subject. Her writing is full of peace and joy.

Yet this book of Sister Elaine is not just about Zen. It is the story of a remarkable woman who is a musician and an artist. She tells us about her childhood in Canada. She relates her experiences in the Philippines and India. But most impressive of all are the moving pages of her book which describe her meditation classes with prisoners in England. Many of her pupils were enlightened and transformed in a way that would have been impossible had they lived in a secure and wealthy environment. We can only hope that her work will continue and that courses in meditation will be offered in prisons throughout the world.

Sister Elaine learned very much in Asia, but she has remained deeply Canadian. Never deracinated, she continues to love her native land. We can be sure that her work will appeal to many Canadians and will open them to a true path to wisdom.

William Johnston S.J.
Tokyo
August 2001

Chapter One

A Circle Is God's Be-Ing

Meister Eckhart

It finally happened: that millennium search for root connections. I was barefoot in the sand dunes on Canada's east coast; barefoot because my Zen studies teach that we can make direct connections through the soles of the feet, and on Canada's coast because of my ancient affinity with the sea. That day, I was being, or as I experienced it then, BE-ING one with the cooling grains inserting themselves between my toes. One with the smell of the sea. One with the waves as they teased both ear and eye to intimacy.

And then suddenly it happened. The connection was made. It was as though my hand had been taken and given a gentle squeeze. I had to smile, understanding why I perceived it all in capital letters. The sacred, the personal, beloved and known. In a flash, I remembered a moment over 25 years before in Japan, when a Japanese Zen Master had confirmed my opening meditative experience, into a world I had never experienced before, a world of no things and no boundaries, but a world at one with my happy pounding heart.

I was invited to write about that realization, and a few days later with pen in hand and almost without thinking, the first words came out . . . "I was born by the sea." Even at the time, I immediately considered that unpremeditated statement. Why did I write it? I knew it came from a truth, but was nevertheless surprised at its immediacy and certainty. And it was not only referring to location, but to experience. And what I experienced was referred to by the *Roshi* (Japanese Zen Master) as a "fact," partly because he was sometimes impatient with my frequent use of the word "mystery." We Christians seem to love that designation and all the baggage it carries. Zen speaks of fact, and a fact is a fact with nothing sticking to it. So those six words were a *fact* for me. I was born by the sea.

I suppose it is to be expected that a Pisces who always likes the feel of moving through water would sooner or later in Zen come upon the *fact* of the water. I found it to be not only a sensuous experience, but the location of the transcendent. There is a *koan* (a riddle the intellect cannot solve), No. 78 in the Blue Cliff Record Book of Koans, which relates that 16 *bodhisattvas* (living saints) came to this experience when they entered the bath. In part it reads:

> In ancient times there were 16 Bodhisattvas. They entered the bath according to the custom of bathing monks at that time. Instantly they realized the "cause" of the water. "All you Zen followers what do you understand?" One said, "Subtle touch, very clear, accomplished Buddhahood dwells here."

So water is eminently a place of rendezvous! I have since discovered that there are many adherents, even some not born under Pisces, who belong to the secret community of sea-intimates. And it is almost commonplace that these protagonists find their life-discipline in meditation. All of them are aware of the connection. It is a kind of home acceptance with the surge of deep waters. Canada's environment-friendly scientist David Suzuki has said that life is animated water. That movement of the sea is, in more ways than one, identical to the deep inner longing and restlessness in the depths of our soul. But it wasn't until three-quarters of a century later that I realized I was born with that longing.

When I lived in England, a friend sent me a copy of George Herbert's poem "The Pulley." In part it reads:

> When God at first made man,
> Having a glass of blessings standing by,
> "Let us," said He, "pour on him all we can.
> Let the world's riches, which dispersed lie,
> contract into a span."
> So strength first made a way;
> Then beauty flowed,
> then wisdom, honour, pleasure.

The poem goes on to say, though, that God purposely withheld one blessing, and that was the gift of satisfaction or complete rest, with the words,

> "Yet let him keep the rest,
> but keep them with repining restlessness."

I was to discover that like my Celtic ancestors, the Japanese people and Oriental spirituality take that repining restlessness for granted. It is contained in the important Japanese word *kokoro,* usually translated "mind." During my time in Japan, it soon became evident to my student colleagues and myself that "mind" was not an appropriate translation of this frequently used Japanese word *kokoro.* Mind is certainly contained in a narrow sense. Eventually, two or three English words were used to indicate a fuller meaning. But in the end, there was still no way to reveal the inherent feeling of *natsukashii* (homesickness or longing), which the Japanese word carries. The Orient seems to be telling us that in our ordinary mind and heart, we have to deal with this longing or bent, as I sometimes like to say. The goal of Zen meditation is to come to an experience of *knowing* what we are longing for. This tells us something of who we are. In my own life, I have come to see that Herbert's "repining restlessness" seems to be involved in our mental processes of coming to want to experience this kind of knowing. I now also know it is true of the sea.

There is a wonderful Oriental story about a little salt doll, which tells us that if we really want to know the sea deeply, then we must go beyond mere intimacy. The doll had the urge to discover the world and went on a journey, experiencing all kinds of new places and adventures. Then one day she came to the edge of the sea and was quite astounded by the restless surging mass of water. "What are you?" she cried. "Touch me and you will find out," answered the sea. So the little salt doll stuck her toe in, and had a truly lovely sensation. But when she withdrew her foot, alas, the toe had disappeared. "What have you done to me?" she cried. "You have given something of yourself in order to understand," the sea replied.

The little salt doll decided that if she really wanted to know the sea, she would have to give more of herself. So next she stuck in her whole foot, and everything up to her ankle disappeared. Surprisingly, in an inexplicable way, she felt very good about it. So she continued going further and further into the sea, losing more and more of her self, all the while understanding the sea more deeply. As a wave broke over the last bit of her, the salt doll was able to cry out, "Now I know what the sea is. It is I."

And here a Zen teacher would want to interject, "What is 'it'?" But I am ahead of my story.

The knowing that the little salt doll came to is not intellectual. It is experiential. Only I can have that experience of *satori* (to know). And I can have it only for myself. It cannot be transmitted. One of the fruits of experiencing it is in feeling one has touched the SACRED, and there arises an immediate desire to use capital letters. The mystics of all religions are wont to resist naming this IT, which is all-embracing, ineffable, absolute, unknowable and unnameable. If I omit the capital letters, I become a teacher (explaining) and not a realized meditator. However, toward the end of the book, as a realized person, I do not use the uppercase because God has become very commonplace and ordinary and an everyday component of my life. To say this is very shocking for innocent souls! So I did not say it.

Another fruit of that wonderful experience is that it is not separate from finding out who I am. In that discovery, I "see" that I am not separate from other beings. At the deepest, we are all ONE. And this type of seeing and knowing brings us to a deeper level of understanding, which is not available to the ordinary state of consciousness. We "see" with what the Oriental masters designate as our "third eye."

Before his death in 1990, my friend the prominent German missioner to the Orient Fr. Hugo Enomiya-Lassalle S.J. used to say that in the great changes which characterize this post-Christian age of ours, we are seeing parallels in our approach to faith. Our seekings and yearnings are now more toward experience than toward the rational. This has led to great interest in Oriental ways and explains why thousands of young Westerners went to the East, and why they continue to make similar journeys today.

Unfortunately, many spiritual seekers thought that Oriental religions were only experience-based and contained no doctrine. This is especially true of Buddhism. In the last century, it has attained an unassailable mystique. This religion which was to become one of the great missionary religions of all time, had as its core the great religious experience of the man known to the Western world as The Buddha. However, in the intervening centuries, his *teachings* have become a great world religion, with its own philosophy and theology and moral teachings. The primary experience is all but forgotten. "What has happened to enlightenment?" is a question that was posed with a certain bluntness by a British author in a recent magazine article about Zen Buddhism practice.

In my youth, I was lucky to have had a gap year between high school and university (1941–42), and I was blessed in many ways, one of which was reading great books. I do not remember any of them dealing in an especially academic way with the East, and yet, from that time on, I knew I was fascinated with the possibilities of the content of the Oriental experience. I thought it would lead to a life-purpose and style that would be just as mysterious and esoteric as *satori* (to see one's own nature). In India, this experience is most often designated by its Sanskrit term, *advaita,* which simply means "not two." I know this tends to make Oriental spirituality sound terribly esoteric. But it isn't. In fact, Zen Masters of old used to peddle their wares as merely "selling water by the river."

This is all old hat now. The exodus to the East by dis-eased Westerners in the 1960s and 1970s has slowed down considerably. We are now at a different stage. We can remain in our Occidental cities, enter a *zendo* (meditation hall), sit cross-legged with others, and descend into the depths of consciousness, even occasionally under a true teacher. Any time we want to indulge in a touch of the Orient, either for silence or a bit of Oriental fascination, we can usually participate in temple ceremonies here on our own soil, often not further away than a streetcar ride. And in these various temples, there seems to be a sincere effort to emulate what happens in the Orient. I cannot speak of all Oriental religions, but in the case of Buddhism, it is generally conceded that most groups, even though well meaning, have started their own version of that religion. The impressive leader of Tibetan Buddhism, the Dalai Lama, has set up remedial classes in Dharamsala for some American self-styled Buddhist monks, who live by their own moral code and tenets of the Buddhist religion and meditation.

Happily, there are several like myself who remain contented to be nourished at Christian altars, and who happily and fruitfully practice legitimate Zen meditation as contemplative prayer. Both are based on silence. The Catholic Church itself spoke clearly at the Second Vatican Council (1962–65) about seeking the truths in other religions, but its representatives have been hot and cold on the subject ever since. In the meantime we practitioners (or sitters, as we say of one another) go on becoming freer in our Zen sitting, believing that we are preparing for the time that this jewel of the Orient finds a true home in the Church.

It is difficult at the moment to see how that is going to happen. We are already witnessing the reluctance of many even to use terms that have reference to the religions of the East. Consequently, the word God has been replaced by a variety of noncommittal names, which people seem to find user-friendly. Ultimate Reality is a favorite. Many spiritual practices, even some that are Christian, speak of relaxation and stress-management as mystical accomplishments! Zen provides another choice. By happy coincidence, the ancient Zen Masters seemed to have been reticent to give only one proper name to the Great Matter. They refer to the Absolute or the Great Reality or even the Infinite. The most commonly used reference though is simply "IT," uttered in humility and respect.

Seven hundred years ago, the great Rhineland Mystic Meister Eckhart said there is no knowing what God is. He and our most prominent mystical theologians refer to God as the great unnameable, the inconceivable Reality. God is beyond even "good," as Eckhart says, so any appendage using IT would apparently concur with Eckhart. In any case, he says we can only describe God by saying what God is not.

It was the Oriental experience of *satori,* of "seeing" IT, that opened for me the deeper way of coming to know that the sea and I are truly one. The happening is certainly gift, coming about when we are enveloped in complete silence, with the intellect not impeding the absolute direct intuitional experience. In other words, when we don't think.

The nonthinking state attained in silence gives our whole being freedom to "do its thing," so to speak. I have heard more than one Zen Master articulate the process as a "giving over" to the Source of the power that animates all of life. We are thus released from the dictates of an imperious ego. And this is true not only in religious pursuits. The international tennis star Pete Sampras says he plays his best tennis when he doesn't think. Of course he is talented and has worked hard to hone his art to the sharpest of edges. But in action, he lets go and gives over to that inner momentum, or more accurately, the Source of that momentum. He admits he doesn't know how it all works. In the Orient, not-knowing is highest wisdom. Sampras would do well in *dokusan,* a private interview with a Zen Master for the purpose of discovering the depth of the participant's practice.

Without a doubt, when I strolled by the sea recently, I was quite aware that there is a kinship between the sea and me. Perhaps I have always been aware of this affinity. I find I liken it to the attraction two drops of rainwater have for each other. Watch them coalesce as they run down a windowpane. Or, more dynamically, as I discovered as a child when I broke two thermometers, two drops of mercury will literally leap at each other if they are brought in close proximity. They have a strong inherent attraction for each other!

When we first become aware of this repining restlessness that longs for union, we see it as an impetus to self-discovery and adventure. Over the years, I have thought of myself as someone on a journey, going to faraway places, heading for a place, or for a teacher, someone following a homeward-oriented map. But in later years as shadows begin to lengthen, I realize I have never left the sand dunes. I had thought I was on a journey, that I was going somewhere. Nothing like a plane ticket around the world to reinforce that illusion. All during my long life, I carried a metaphoric pocketful of sea to various destinations around the world. At one memorable moment in a faraway country, I tasted "It," to use the Oriental term. More specifically, IT tasted IT, and what had been a relationship deepened toward identification. In one sense I had arrived. In another, I had never left. This book is an exploration of the meaning of these experiences.

My millennium insight brought it all into focus. I had realized long before who the little salt doll is, but the knowing has deepened. There is something about the sea that pulls one into its depth, although that something remains unrevealed. It cannot be seen but is that whereby the eye can see (Kena Upanishad). When I made a rough Atlantic crossing by liner in October 1953, I was certainly aware of the hidden power of the ocean. The crew had roped off much of the main deck, and as I stood unsteadily clutching the thick cords, the ship seemed very small as it was pulled into the hollow of the wave and then catapulted to the crest. I thought the ship seemed built to use that power, not fight it. Nor did I fight it. I let it carry me along and up and down. It was many years and hundreds of adventures later that I would articulate that happening accurately.

When I was about 10 years of age, I found a volume of the writings of the distinguished scholastic philosopher Thomas Aquinas. I had been born on what was once celebrated as his feast day (a date that has since changed) and subsequently informed of his mental prowess and scholastic writings. That day in a religious bookstore in Moncton, New Brunswick, I saw a thick volume entitled *Aquinas,* and rather excitedly, I flipped the book open for the first taste of my famous patron saint. That particular page treated the five ways of demonstrating the existence of God. Pretty heavy stuff for a 10-year-old! But I read the full paragraph. I recall it spoke of seeing movement everywhere, each one proceeding from a previous movement. In the last sentence of that paragraph, Aquinas proclaimed the prime mover is called God! My young soul could only grasp that much, and I slammed the book shut. Although very young at the time, I was able to absorb something of that wisdom, and have held the insight of God as power, as it were, through the many succeeding years. God, the world, and the 10,000 — or however many — things in it, all became verbs! This eventually brought validation to my findings in Oriental mysticism.

Often when I speak of spirituality, instead of noun forms such as "We receive our life from the sacred Power within," I think and express myself using verbs: "We allow the inner Sacred Power to en-lifen us." That seems closer to me to what's happening. The noun form suggests a one-off event. To be en-lifened is an on-going happening. And to say en-lifeing is truest to my experience. When I allow that power to simply *be* (another verb) then I am in synch with *IT.* Then I see myself as truly Be-ing, which *has* to be a verb! And thus I come to describe a true contemplative.

The mystic Eckhart has stripped the articulation to its very bones: do nothing, let God do everything. No different, perchance, from my adventure of endeavouring to study *shodo* (calligraphy writing) in Japan. My teacher started by explaining the inner Source which must empower the shoulder, arm, hand, brush and ink to write. I was to banish all ego and effort, and just give over to that power. I was to begin by simply doodling. My efforts brought only recriminations from my teacher. "You are using ego and muscle!" or perhaps "*You* are doing the writing." Two years later the doodling had not improved, the teacher saying the flow was still blocked. I quit in the third year. Calligraphy didn't seem to be my path of becoming a mystic!

It wasn't until later and 20 years of *zazen* and violin playing that brought me to the point where the Zen Master was able to say after Larry McGarrell (my Jesuit accompanist) and I had played some Brahms, "You have finally got yourself out of the way. " He didn't mean it particularly as a compliment. For him it was a fact. The way things should be. And one famous violinist, when asked how he managed to play the Beethoven concerto so beautifully, used almost the same words: "I have splendid music, a splendid instrument, a splendid bow. All I have to do is bring them together and get out of the way."

And so that other day at the beach, taking a handful of sand, and letting it slowly stream through my fingers, I felt I was Be-ing in the deepest sense. I was at peace with the enclosing circle my life is becoming. Granted, the 34 years in the Orient is perhaps the high point of learning in the journey. It is certainly the aspect that people find most interesting.

I looked out at the sea, too, that companion of a lifetime. For a moment I saw right across to the Isle of Mull, where my Scottish ancestor Flora MacInnes must have also stood contemplating the ocean's fearful mystery. I breathed a grateful breath that she had found the courage to set sail with her two young sons, and without the husband who had recently died. I could only guess the ups and downs of her years in Cape Breton. I pray that she too eventually found "the world is full of gold" (a literal translation of a line from *koan* 17 of the Blue Cliff Record) and no different from those four wonderful lines by William Blake, from his "Ideas of Good and Evil":

> To see a world in a grain of sand,
> And a heaven in a wild flower;
> Hold Infinity in the palm of your hand,
> And eternity in an hour.

Chapter Two

Before the Earth Came into Being

I was born by the sea. I also have another beginning, with which I have been in touch for many years. When former Prime Minister Pierre Trudeau died, Canadians from coast to coast to coast mourned his passing, and the extensive radio and television coverage of the event allowed us to discover many heretofore unknown facets of his life. The one I would like to comment on here is the fact that apparently he used to read parts of the Bible to his sons regularly, because he wanted them to be in touch with their roots. Our roots! We Christians have a story, a delightful one, with roots in the evolving Jewish religion, a boy-child being born at a time that came to be known as the start of the Common Era, an attractive biographical narrative of his ideals and exploits for a short 30 years, his astounding resurrection from the dead, followed by a mission explosion to all corners of the world.

A record of the beginnings of our story is contained in the Bible's Book of Proverbs. We use it as one of our *zendo* (meditation hall) chants:

The wisdom of God says this
You created me when your purpose first unfolded.
From the oldest of your works
From everlasting I was firmly set,
From the beginning, before the earth came into being.
The deep was not when I was born.
There were no springs to gush with water.
Before the hills I came to birth.
Before you made the earth, the countryside
Or the first grains of the world's dust.
When you fixed the heavens firm I was there.
When you drew a ring on the surface of the deep.
When you thickened the clouds above,
When you assigned the seas its boundaries
And the waters will not invade the shore.
When you laid down the foundations of the world,
I was by your side, a master craftsman,
Delighting you day after day,
Ever at play in your presence
At play everywhere in your world,
Delighting to be with the children of the earth.

(Proverbs 8:22-31)

Mystical language indeed. Who are our mystics today? Yamada Roshi (my Zen Master in Kamakura) used to tell his disciples in Japan that every human being is born to be a mystic. One day at Wormwood Scrubs Prison in London, England, after a particularly good first meditation with 24 lifers, we all just sat there in a peaceful kind of silence, not wanting to disturb that place which had brought us together. Eventually I spoke and dared to quote that statement I had heard my teacher say any number of times, that everybody is born to be a mystic. Two or three of the lifers nodded in assent, and there wasn't a snicker of disbelief in the group. Each in his own way seemed to know what I was talking about.

Yes, we are all born to be mystics, and I seem to understand there is a mysticism of light and a mysticism of darkness. Rilke says: "God speaks to each of us as he makes us. Then walks with us silently into the night." And in another poem he says,

You darkness, of whom I am born
I love you more than all the fires
that fence in the world,
for the fire makes
a circle of light for everyone,
and then no one outside learns of you.

But the darkness pulls in everything,
shapes and fires, animals and myself.
How easily it gathers them.
Powers and people
and it is possible a great energy
is moving near me.
I have faith in nights.[1]

Buddhism is at home in the darkness. Zen speaks of its mystics as being blind because they see nothing or, as I like to spell it, no-thing. It is of course a nothingness full of potential! Christianity is a religion of light and joy. "You are the light of the world"(Mt 5:13-14). "I have come that your joy may be complete." It is known as the religion of love, which is very appealing. Still, the number of adherents who subscribe to those gifts appears to be dwindling by the day. What is happening and why?

I sometimes ask myself, "Where am I in my religion?" To which I reply with the enigmatic Oriental response, "I don't know." And that is not ignorance. In the Orient I discovered we do not have to know everything all of the time. Indeed, there are things which are not meant to be known or understood. That does not mean we cannot accept them. Religion, which is meant to tie us back to our roots, is not all

---

[1] Note: All sources are identified in the list of books consulted, at the end of the book.

black and white. I feel I belong in the one holy catholic apostolic Church, but wherever I live I do search around until I find a priest and community amongst whom I feel at home. When I lived in England I noted that there were nine Catholic churches in and around Oxford, where I attended mass, listened to sermons, and spoke with people in the various congregations. Eventually I settled on Blackfriars, where I found the authentic reality I needed. Each Sunday there is a popular 9:30 family mass where participants are welcomed from all over the area. Although traditionally dioceses encourage Catholics to worship in their own parish churches, Blackfriars has no parish limits. As a result, we tend to form a somewhat like-minded community. Sometimes the Blackfriars' mass gets a little noisy as families often can be, but the participants are friendly, and there's an open invitation for me to participate in the little orchestras that accompany the music. Sermons are almost always informative and pithy, sometimes even humorous. I feel at home there. It's real.

Wherever I have lived, my parish, my religious and spiritual home, has always been important for me. I grew up in the attractive small Maritime city of Moncton, its population about 30,000 in my day, and claimed by my mother to be a city of stately elms, until the Dutch disease overtook them. She presided over the house at 187 Botsford Street, the architecture of which she drafted, even to the point of supervising the excavation at a stone quarry for the exact design of the living room fireplace. And down the elm-lined road was the rather beautiful stone church under the patronage of St. Bernard. I was born just after the pastor Monsignor Savage returned from the Holy Land, bringing back water of the Jordan River. I and several other newborns were baptized with that water from the river where Christ had been baptized two millennia before. My parents of course were delighted with the event, and generally speaking, our family was comfortable in our Catholic religion. My parents, brother, two sisters and I occupied most of pew 93 in the church every Sunday.

Today, I remember two things about St. Bernard's church: the organ, and the teaching we received there. The organ is a Cassavant, made in Quebec; the diapason for mellifluous sounds were well used and the pulsating tremolo added in generous measure. I loved it then and do still. Great classical masterpieces like the Bach Preludes and Fugues are perhaps best served on European brand organs, which produce a simple, direct tone, but for warm, soft, endearing colors touching the heart during mass, or a wedding, or indeed a funeral, there's nothing like a Cassavant. A couple of years ago I attended a funeral in north Toronto, and before the service began, the organist kept us company with such familiar delectables as Vaughan Williams' *Greensleeves* and Elgar's *Nimrod*. I suddenly realized I was listening to old familiar tones rather than well-known tunes. Sure enough, upon investigation following the service, the young organist told me that the instrument he was playing *was* a Cassavant.

During my gap year between high school and university I sang in the choir. It was then I realized how suited Latin sounds are for the human voice in producing beautiful tone. Of course we sang some hymns in English, but for the expected "internal lift" to come frequently and deeply, lots of vowel sounds are necessary. All this came back to me as, with the rest of Canada, I listened to the choir singing the *Lachrimosa* from Mozart's *Requiem* at Pierre Trudeau's funeral in Montreal's Notre Dame Basilica. This church music is truly magnificent! Many people echoed my own feelings, that the two-hour mass, awash with tears of grieving and gratitude, appropriate and effective actions in the sanctuary, and readings performed slowly and movingly, gave us occasion to taste of our roots indeed. Time and again we heard or read remarks that something heartwarming and home-coming had been found as people watched the graceful movements of those officiating in the sanctuary, smelled the mystical fragrance of the incense and red roses and heard the kind of message articulated by the speakers of a full life lived with great passion and nourished by meditation. This sumptuousness was extended in the warmth and grandeur of the church architecture, the liturgy adjoining our senses and the earthly throne of God, all the things the heart needed to soften the edges of the sorrow. We came away with our sense of exile assuaged, realizing again that our culture and religion had evolved a kind of ceremony that gives not only an appropriate final farewell to a unique fellow sojourner, but also addresses the repining restlessness in our hearts, identified with its very Source. Justin Trudeau's *"Je t'aime, Papa"* not only honored the earthly father, but pointed us all to our destiny. "Good to see the ol' incense smoking around again!" "Oh, that music!" Have we *really* forgotten our story? Today we are said to be in exile. But is this true?

We are living in a post-Christian era. What has happened to the Church and religion? Or are we merely still on pilgrimage into new tomorrows? Of course there were moments of dis-ease when I was young. I recall my father remembering as we entered the church one Sunday morning that he had had to take medicine at 4 a.m. He went to the vestry to inquire whether that had broken his fast. He was told yes, and thus was not allowed to receive communion. I remember thinking there was something unfair there. Too much legalism. But he accepted it.

Over the ensuing years, many have not accepted that legalistic authority. It was with rejoicing that I learned of the far-reaching possibilities of Vatican II, which were available to us about 1965, during my early years in Japan, and the two issues which have stayed with me: (a) for each individual human being, the deepest authority is one's own informed conscience and (b) we were encouraged to search out and use the truths and goodness held in other religions. I guess in some ways I'm a bit of a reductionist. I imbibed those two facets well, and have tried to live by them ever since. This has kept me happy and responsible, too, I think. I am kept alive by the truth, beauty, goodness and contemplation I find in some religions, including my own. And I find a certain peace and its completion from and with the inner Presence.

When Pete Sampras won his 7th Wimbledon and 14th Grand Slam title, he publicly thanked God and said, "I couldn't have done it without help from upstairs." Michael Jordan would refer to the goal of his sport as "Sacred Hoops," the book with this title becoming a bestseller. These are two famous athletes who apparently recognize the nature of their connections. But what has happened to so many of my other fellow sojourners and friends and relatives? Most of my nieces and nephews don't "go to church." Often they are exemplary citizens, great parents, ardent athletes with vital ecological concerns. But they shudder when church is mentioned. And it seems to be the microcosm of a greater disdain, that of religion. Some seem to find it all irrelevant and sometimes ask the question, "Do we need religion at all?"

People are adrift in mainline Christian churches. I have just returned to live in Canada after an absence of 40 years, and am not yet in full understanding of what is transpiring here. When in Japan, I found a like concern in the Buddhist Temples there. Yamada Roshi used to proclaim that Japanese Buddhism was dying. He felt it had answered his needs during his lifetime, but saw it as failing those of his children. He used to say, if a religion is failing its people, then it deserves to die.

My friend and colleague Dr. David Loy, a Buddhist philosopher who lives in Kamakura, feels that Buddhism will not go the fundamentalist route as some Christian sects seem to be doing. It is true that some forms, like Soka Gakkai and

Rissho Koseikai, tend to go in that direction, but he says the greater problem for Buddhism in Asia is irrelevance, and that it doesn't function at all or at all well in the new world. The traditional forms seem superstitious to educated people and therefore something you grow out of as you modernize. Since the very beginning of Buddhism's missionary travels, it reached only the elite, which means that it was associated with nationalistic aims, promoting the welfare and security of the country. Therefore, the older traditional forms of Buddhism could be in for a rough time. But, curiously, in more sophisticated modern forms of Buddhism there is a resurgence of interest among the educated elite, in such countries as Singapore, Malaysia and Thailand. David thinks there is considerable hope for the future of a more enlightened and demythologized Buddhism among the educated young people, which he has experienced right in Japan.

Whatever is transpiring today in the religious field, it is nevertheless apparent that the paradigm shift predicted by leaders in many fields seems indeed to be coming to pass, especially in human consciousness. Some say this is as great a move as our ancestors' shift ages ago from a simple animal-like consciousness to the beginnings of our present self-reflective consciousness. Some Christians are earnestly involved in a spiral of courage and participation. Others are not.

Tom Harpur of the *Toronto Star* points to the phenomenon of big, bulging "super-churches" in the suburbs, filled with bright-faced conservative evangelicals and their offspring, which for him provides a real puzzler, the rapid growth of ultra-conservative denominations and groups. He feels in this era of relentless change and anxiety that many cannot cope with it all, and find it easier to accept simple, black-and-white, straight-from-God-and-history-book answers that fundamentalist groups of all religions serve up on demand: an instant security, a cessation of doubts and the inevitable high that comes with belonging at last to the elect.

Reading that made me wonder, what has happened to our sense of freedom? What has happened to dreams? Do we no longer want and yearn? Do we not wander down the nights and down the days fleeing the pursuit of the hound of heaven? Those freedoms were bought for us at a stiff price. Are we to squander our inheritance?

The well-known author, lecturer and Old Testament teacher Walter Brueggemann also says we have forgotten our own story. But I tend to think the story is moving on to another chapter. I think the same archetypes are at work, whether we realize it or not. And those archetypes are working, sowing and reaping in a new field. My life experience has been that we have entered a new paradigm shift where it seems cosmology is overtaking theology as our most popular point of reference. In England, the most densely booked seminars deal with science, mysticism and ecology, with the occasional reference to feminism. I have come as a matter of procedure to expect scientists to write on mysticism, ecologists to write on mysticism, and religious writers to include all three.

My concern is the quality of the presentations: not only their authenticity, but also the articulation. Some written stuff on mysticism is pretty woolly, though sometimes wittily clothed in humor. My friend the Canadian philosopher Ernie McCullough was invited by a well-known meditation group to become a teacher. They promised to confirm him as such within a three-month period. In disbelief, he pointed to the fact that it took me 18 years. The retort perhaps said it all: "Some people travel by plane. Others by donkey." Ernie also related the popularity of the well-known joke about the Buddhist nun who approached a hot dog stand and is asked how she would like her hot dog. "Make me one with everything" was the knowing reply.

Another concern is that even among the sincere, many are content with dabbling. By dabbling I mean working from a theoretical basis, reading or writing about mysticism and not practising it. I suppose the hundreds whom I have taught in my various *zendos* represent those with fire in the belly. Those interested in moving out of the head and into the spirit. Our best hope is perhaps with them. Without diminishing the gifts of the old order, a new emphasis is being addressed; new invitations were and are being felt in the heart where mysticism begins. As yet, thankfully there are not too many rules and signposts, despite the occasional word of caution from the Vatican.

Amongst these few souls, there is a new inner freedom and confidence which comes from the inner Source of freedom and confidence itself. Every particle of creation is filled with God! It is not in other hands. I think of the outstanding Canadian novelist Robertson Davies having Parlabane warn: "Be not another." And paradoxically, Zen would tell us in a certain sense that we *are* all others!

One of the starting points of this impetus seems to have been scientific. I probably belonged to the generation that read Fritjof Capra's *Tao of Physics* as though he were saying "our thing." His enthusiasm for Buddhist texts, of course, won me over to whatever he and some of his colleagues had to say about their scientific findings. I have not eschewed their critics, and admit my ignorance about quantum physics, but I read his books avidly, probably because so much of what they say about the nature of subatomic particles seems friendly to what I know of the Oriental religious experience. Is this a paradox, and am I its center? I feel I can discern something of science from its theory, but I am at a loss to understand how scientists can discern mysticism by theory.

Some theologians of the last century, such as Karl Rahner and Martin Buber, expressed their mystical experiences well. They have even given us many signposts for the future. But with no close second, the first word of mystics after an experience has to do with origin. I cited my own declaration that I had been born by the sea. For others, the expression goes beyond the physical self.

Sometime during my years in Kamakura, a German colleague acquainted me with the later writings of Karl Rahner. He was already established as a solid and safe theologian in the Church. At some later point, he seems to have had a mystical experience; his writings then took on new depth and revelation. I was delighted that Rahner, too, returning to the world of time and space after an experience, immediately spoke of his eternal birth. I assembled some of his thoughts and paraphrased them as follows:

> Our beginning is hidden in God. It is decided. Only when we have arrived will we fully know what our origin is. For God is mystery as such, and what he posited when he established us in our beginning, is still the mystery of his free will. But without evacuating the mystery, we can say that there belongs to our beginning, all that is there, everything whatsoever that exists, and is silently concentrated in the wellspring of our own existence, and all the rest is pervaded by what each is in himself, and therefore as a beginning posited by God, uniquely and unrepeatedly.[2]

Rahner excludes nothing:

> (It resides) with what is hard and what is easy, delicate and harsh, with what belongs to the abyss and what is heavenly. All is encompassed by God, his knowledge and his love. All has to be accepted. And as we advance towards it all, we

---

[2] References to Rahner's work were translated and paraphrased by the author

experience everything, one thing after another, until future and origin coincide.

And Rahner brings Christ into the history of our beginning:

One thing about this beginning, however, has been said to us by the Word of God. The possibility of acceptance itself belongs to the might of the divinely deposited beginning. And if we accept, we accept sheer love and happiness. And the more that love and forgiveness which encompasses and belongs to our beginning is accepted in the pain of life, and in the death which gives life, and the more this element emerges and is allowed to manifest itself and pervade our history, the more difference, the contradiction is resolved and redeemed.

And finally Rahner moves into what I term "identification."

All the more will it be revealed that we ourselves were also implied in that pure beginning. When the beginning has found itself in the fulfilment and has been fulfilled in the freedom of accepting love, GOD WILL BE ALL IN ALL.

This revealing aggregate of Rahner's experience has proved very helpful for many of my disciples. Indeed, it seems to have been what they termed "the missing link." They had somehow lost the connection with their Christian roots as they felt called to explore the treasure house of Oriental spirituality.

Of course the famous '60s was the turning point in the last century. Why? I think many of us felt the need to answer or follow the "lean in our heart," that Celtic longing. Some of us touched the treasure, and came down from our mountain of experience, partially freed, cleansed, detached. We found no need to condemn, slaughter and bury the old, as we endeavored to own our past while being true to our new vision. If I am an example of at least some of them, I feel we have profited enormously by our experience. It has somehow been consistent with the ache in the heart. I know I echoed Yamada Roshi's own saying when I came to experience: "My teachers have not deceived me!" It's a happy heart, "ever at play in God's presence, at play everywhere in God's world, delighting to be with the children of the earth," as Proverbs has it.

Perhaps we "touchers-in-mysticism" are the forerunners of what is to come in the paradigm shift. What we have found is perhaps best contained in the phrase "my true self." Unfortunately it has become so hackneyed I hesitate to use it. "To find our true self." That glimpse/touch/discovery, especially if it is in-depth, is an experience of revelation and joy in which we find ourselves at one with that which we are experiencing. So that we can truly say, "This is I. I am not separate. I belong." I myself never felt inclined to name this discovery as "my true self," but today it seems to be the favorite description of the experience.

The Oriental Masters have always declared the religious nature of the *satori/advaita* experience. Yamada Roshi dreamed of it becoming part of the mystical treasure house of the Christian Church. But I must admit I cannot see this happening in my lifetime.

Although I understand why many people are rightly critical, I myself do not feel an adversary to the present-day Church, despite its problems in authority and procrastination. I do not condone some of its wayward members and their teachings, especially the drivel of some Sunday sermons, but then there are other churches I can choose to attend. I find I have a home in my heart for the Christian communities. I find many people still concerned about religion, whether in or out of religious life. On the other hand, we must admit that the old days are certainly gone.

When I slip into pew 93 of St. Bernard's in Moncton these days, I remember the second reason I felt grounded there: the teaching I received. The Cassavant plays on, the potential of my emotive memory takes over, and I enumerate again the gifts of that gap year in my youth. Gone are the holistic, eloquent sermons of the late pastor Msgr. Roy MacDonald, but my understanding works gloriously now because he whetted my appetite with grounded and informed knowledge from his top-class intellect, his vision of a cohesive world and its creatures, his integration of the cosmos, the personal and the divine. I ate hungrily at his table and am grateful for the means he gave me to form the habit of discerning. Each class with Msgr. MacDonald started with an analysis of the week's historical and political events, which were then related to the Church's teaching and our own personal lives. I was grateful not only for the sharing of his scholarship, but also for the display of pure enthusiasm and love for his work as a teacher. His influence endures, even now. I do not belittle the need for role models for the young today, which is a popular hue and cry, but I wonder sometimes if perhaps even more importantly teenagers suffer from the lack of inspiring teachers.

As I reflect, I also see the enormous potential for growth and maturity in my own teenage adventures of fun and sports and the first squeaks of human love. Memories of beautiful snowfalls, sleigh rides, basketball games, dances, movies, and a town full of airmen (Moncton had five air bases during the Second World War, and our home was well visited by enlisted men). Mother, three daughters, good food and music, all providing a feminine touch to the masculine, military predominance of life at that time and place. That era also provided each of us with our first taste of death. One of the surrounding air force depots was a flying training center, and accidents and death were frequent occurrences. I remember my older sister, Olwin, having a date with a charming piano-playing officer. He never arrived that evening. She discovered later that he had been killed earlier in the day in a flying accident. That was a very sobering experience for the whole family, and every airman who stepped over our threshold was henceforth received gratefully. We were also mindful of our brother, Bill, who was serving overseas in the Canadian army.

And so my two sisters and I moved along with the times, and our interests and lives touched eternal as well as more mundane issues. And as I reminisce, I see in parallel that the Church's theology has had to move out of the staid institutional environment and enter the living elements of creation itself. God's revelation is contained not only in holy books, but in the unfolding process of the universe itself. As Diarmuid O'Murchu says in *Religion in Exile:* "We cannot access it in academic detail but we can begin to contemplate something of its mysterious elegance" (p. 225).

In time I grew to love the Oriental teaching that contemplation is the work of the third eye, often represented in Oriental statues with a precious jewel in the centre of the forehead. The Third Eye does not look to the outside; rather, it looks within, for the first of our sightings. One of the sages from the Orient, Dogen Zenji, seems to say that with a little help from beyond, we can come to experience the Divine Indwelling. It seems to me that religion will make a lot more sense to people today if they have touched the Ultimate Reality in actual experience, as well as in their ordinary, everyday lives. I recall the Oxford Dominican Bob Ombres commiserating with exhausted parents in a post-Christmas sermon, suggesting with the words that every bow tied during the Yule season can be a point of transcendence.

And the best news of that experience is to discover we are not separate from that inner Splendor. This happening/experience in Japanese is *satori*, which is the noun form of the verb *satoru,* "to know." There are several words available in that language that indicate the kind of knowing referred to. *Satori* is not intellectual, it is not history, it is not only for an elite. It is a knowing available to all, at our deepest level, where we find no-thing but a perception of the most ancient beauty and goodness and truth. We find our knowing is a touch of a unity which already exists, and can become operative in our lives. It is the kind of knowing expressed by Robert Browning:

to know
consists in opening out a way
whence the imprisoned Splendour may escape

Chapter Three

Becoming Free in the Body

I walked every day to language school in Kyoto, in full view of Mount Hiei, overlooking the ancient city. I had some unfinished business with that mountain. Indirectly, it had saved my vocation.

I had a difficult time in Our Lady's Missionaries (OLM) novitiate, which was situated in the Scottish district of Glengarry, near Ottawa, Ontario. First the physical adjustment. The routine seemed deadening for a free spirit. Perhaps that was the rationale, killing the urge to be elsewhere. I missed the freedom to plan and buy a long train ticket. In those days, you bought tickets portion by portion on a long, narrow strip. Moncton to Montreal would be the first portion, then Montreal to Toronto, then Toronto to Winnipeg, etc., with perforations for demarcation lines. Eighteen or twenty inches held the promise of much adventure!

Then there was the confining enclosure of being dressed in a religious habit. Because our congregation was founded as late as 1949, it did not have the elegant flourishes many of the old communities still sported. Even so, ours was designed for the same purpose, namely to conceal both the feminine figure and a woman's crown and glory, her hair. Our dress consisted of a semi-fitted bodice and skirt, topped by a circular cape from neck to waist. The head piece was a small roll of white linen that framed the upper half of the face, to which a veil was pinned to hide the hair.

Early in the 1960s, I went to the Manhattanville School of Religious Music on Upper Manhattan Island for a summer course in religious music. At that time Rodgers and Hammerstein were composing *The Sound of Music*. Richard Rodgers came out to the school one day with some of his colleagues, to hear our music and also to study the variety of religious dress worn by nuns from different religious orders. The School's principal, Mother Morgan, chose about 10 of us for his perusal, assuring me that he would like ours best, it was so simple and modern. Of course just the opposite was true. Rogers and his colleagues wanted something flamboyant and eye-catching. OLM simplicity didn't stand a chance!

We had received the habit when postulancy ended and novitiate began. Even at the beginning, I hated the feel of it. It was more binding than the religious vows I was studying. I remember being awake almost all night before receiving the long black habit. I would look at it hanging there beside my cot, and wonder how I would ever be able to wear it. That was June 25, 1954.

After the Second Vatican Council ended in 1965, when the Church and religious life were gasping for a breath of fresh air, we debated the issue of continuing with the habit. One consideration was that it is very popular with Native people on our various missions. This did not cut much ice with me, so (being in Japan at the time) I asked the opinion of my violin pupils and their mothers, with whom I did a lot of work. Their preference was based on appearances. They said the habit looked so nice when I was kneeling at the altar rail! I personally felt it was a wall between me and the Japanese, a wall I was trying to demolish. When the time came for us to change, I decided to follow the advice of certain psychological suggestions I had read about. I took the pieces of linen that had bound my head, cut them up into little pieces with a pair of scissors and then watched them burn to ashes. Finally I was rid of that particular habit.

The change to street-length clothes was dramatic. It took place shortly after the Vatican II documents were implemented, about 1966, when I was still in Japan. The directive from our motherhouse in Toronto was that we had to wear hats when not in the convent. There wasn't a tam-o-shanter nun in our Japan group. We all chose a hat fit for a Buckingham Palace garden party! Pictures of that era are a source of great merriment now. My first mission apostolate was to help found a culture center in the Osaka suburb of Suita. The first day I wore "lay" clothes there, I couldn't believe the scratching noises emanating from my pupil's wee violin, as I accompanied him. When I turned around to look, he had the bow *under* the strings rather than on top. He was unable to look at the music at all because he couldn't keep his eyes off my clothing.

Shortly afterward, when I visited our tuberculosis hospital in Maizuru on the Japan Sea, as I paused between the cots in the women's ward, I felt a soft tickling on my scalp. I turned around and found one of the younger women patients standing on her bed, parting my hair. She said she had never seen a blonde before and wondered if the color were black down at the roots. I assured her it made me happy to have my hair back again, and with her perceptive Oriental feminine intuition she murmured, *"Soooo desu ne!"* ("That's so, isn't it!")

There were other difficulties in novitiate, too. I knew that I was on a search and that I was a seeker, but for what? Because I was a violinist by profession, my life had taken shape with an ideal and a goal that were much easier to define than the ideals presented in religious life! Now looking back almost 50 years, I find it easier to articulate. The fine painter Alex Colville, whose artistic roots are also at my alma mater, Mount Allison University, recently quoted the novelist Vladimir Nabokov, who described the aspiration of an artist as "the shadow of an object that is not yet present." He presented it as the genesis of a creative idea. It certainly rings true to me about my beginnings in religious life.

Then one day, someone put into my hands a copy of the book *One with Jesus* by the Belgian Jesuit Paul de Jaegher. I knew immediately with gut certitude that that was the first indication of what the future would be for me. I had had a few romantic dreams of the possibilities of being a missioner, but they gave way during the humdrum novitiate to a deeper impulse, as did all my doubts when I found de Jaegher's book. It did not have the answers yet. Just the direction.

De Jaegher tells his own story about his desire as a priest to become intimate with God. Intimacy demands two, and he seemed to find his humanity getting in the way. He does not say how it happened, but suddenly he came to realize that it was not only intimacy God wanted of him, but rather identification through experience. I see now it was the leap from relationship to experiential knowing. Henceforth he took the Pauline phrase literally. He developed a spirituality based on the text "I live now not I, but Christ lives within me" (Galatians 2:20). The Jerusalem Bible's translation is even more pointed: "I live now not with my own life, but with the life of Christ who lives in me."

The Jesuit did not give specific directions on how he practiced this spirituality, but his book is full of encouragement.

I tried a few experiments on my own, but they all went through the thinking process, which I soon discovered was creating an objective twosome. I did, however, have my own inspired insight, that the secret or core of that teaching lay in the two words "not I."

The other insight at that time concerned the type of meditation I had been taught as a postulant, one based on the Ignatian method. This uses a scriptural quotation, to be worked on by our various mental abilities. In novitiate, we were given this quote at the end of night prayers the previous evening. In the early morning, we would consider what was quoted, who said it, where it was said, etc. And we would then imagine ourselves being present during the encounter. Finally we were to express our feelings about what took place during the imagined encounter.

I took this exercise very seriously. Just like the popular Cistercian writer Thomas Merton did in his early monastic training, I wrote out in longhand the content of my daily meditation. Many people were greatly influenced by his 1948 autobiography *The Seven Storey Mountain*. I know I found it powerful in content and presentation, as do many people even today. I don't recall that I endeavored to emulate Merton in any way, but I did take time each day in novitiate to write out the morning meditation as I remembered it, and in due time would give my notes to the Novice Mistress for her perusal. In most other areas of training, she and I were not on the best of terms. She would occasionally give a concealed hint that I might not have a vocation. Shortly after entering I celebrated my 30th birthday. Most of the other novices had entered at an early age, and were probably more amenable to formation and change.

The Novice Mistress took great interest in my determination to learn how to meditate. She bought many books for me, which I dutifully read. None had the impact that de Jaegher's *One with Jesus* would later have on me. At the same time, she was uneasy that I was becoming singular, and I had to battle it out with her as to the extent that she could encourage this. For instance, one day she spoke of a retreat being preached to a local group of contemplative nuns by an eminent prayer master. She gave it long consideration, but eventually decided against allowing me to participate, because it was not open to the other novices. So I ploughed on alone, noticing that my meditations were becoming less colorful, less people populated, and less wordy. I saved the nightly scriptural reading for study, and I just sat still in company with Jesus during the actual meditation time. No more writings. I was becoming more and more inwardly content.

Even knowing that I was probably in the right place with Our Lady's Missionaries, and feeling that there was indeed Nabokov's shadow of an object not yet present, the discipline of taming a spirit prone to activity did not come easily. So many people think a vocation to religious life is a pillar of fire in the desert or a voice from on high. Despite what others have said or predicted, I entered because I felt called. Just that. No fireworks. But I knew that calling had something to do with the "lean in the heart/the shadow of an object." Still pretty nebulous stuff for someone who revelled in symphony orchestras and adventure, sports and friends, out of doors and travelling.

I never tried to talk myself out of the presence of this inner longing, and kept believing that the shadow would reveal itself to me and assuage that longing. That first Christmas in the convent, my younger sister, Ethel, sent a recording of the Brahms Violin Concerto as played by Ida Haendel. The rendition was satisfying and was my sole classical companion for three years. I was allowed to practise violin every day for 30 minutes between the bunk beds in the novitiate, and rather frequently played Scottish melodies for the founder of our congregation, Msgr. Donald Ranald MacDonald. I even wrote a medley of Scottish tunes for the fiddle-playing rector of the Alexandria Cathedral to perform at Robbie Burns' celebrations.

And of course there are countless humorous incidents always happening in a novitiate. My companion in crime was a local lassie, Penny MacIntosh. For our daily adventure, one of us would collect the unconsecrated wine left over in the cruet at the end of mass to store in a bottle hidden in the vestry. This was possible under the nonjudgmental eye of a more senior novice, Mona Kelly, who typed every morning in the vestry. On Friday mornings at 11:50, Penny and I would meet behind the furnace in the basement and share the week's bounty, never more than a couple of mouthfuls each, careful to follow the orgy with a swallow of milk as well. Penny believed it would hide the smell of the wine as we sat for lunch in the communal dining room at 12:00.

As her name suggests, Penny came from Scottish stock and we had many sessions together as I played the Keel Row to her Highland fling. She was missioned to Africa, where she developed cancer. She was brought home for surgery, and although unconscious most of the time, when I took my fiddle to her bedside, she wiggled her toes noticeably during a rendition of her last Straspey and favorite lament. She died in her 33rd year, and was OLM's only death in the 52 years of our existence. Mona Kelly served in Africa, Mozambique, and is still going strong in Brazil. She was recently awarded the Order of Canada for her outstanding compassion. Penny and I had been recipients of that virtue some 45 years earlier.

Despite the fun in novitiate, I was constantly starved intellectually. I can recall only one book that came to us that interested me. One of the novices had received a copy of Jacques Maritain's book on philosophy and the arts. Of course, newspapers and novels were not allowed, but I picked up more than one bit of news of friends in the musical world as I slowly spread papers on the kitchen floor I had just scrubbed.

Our religious training was meager. Those ancient spiritual practices were far more humorous than enlightening. The gem I recall most vividly is the story of the reformed prostitute who taught the glories of God by extracting worms from her ulcerating breasts, which turned into pearls as she handed them to the unbelieving. And conversely there was the hungry novice who tried to steal a lettuce leaf from the convent garden only to have it sprout a devil as it neared her mouth!

Mercifully, over the three-year period, I was given a couple of books that met expectations of what I wanted to do in religious life. The first was by Janet Erskine Stewart, a Scottish nun of the Sacred Heart Congregation. Her approach to novitiate difficulties was common sense. In one of her letters to a struggling novice she says:

> These things that come home to us and hurt our self-love and humble us in the dust, these are some of God's best graces, full of promise, and to think you are at the end of them. There will come more revelations even more humbling, ever more humbling, ever more intimate and ever more true. True. But never let them cast you down. Remember they are birthdays, the putting away of the things of a child. And your vocation beaten by storms, will come out all the truer.

On the way home to Canada on leave after the first six years in Japan, I travelled via Europe and gratefully visited the grave of Mother Stewart at Roehampton Convent in London, England. The need to express my gratitude was real.

The other important book was a life of the Jesuit missioner to the Orient, Francis Xavier. The book presented him as a most attractive figure, happily strolling along the narrow streets of old Kyoto juggling three or four apples, to the delight of a group of children following him. The worst of his days in Japan were spent trying to gain access to Mount Hiei, to meet with the monks there. Xavier had come to see that the real power in the country was held not by an Emperor or Shogun, but by the Buddhist priests and monks inhabiting the 1,500 temples on the beautiful mountain overlooking the city. I felt his frustration at never being able to gain access. One desperate afternoon as a Junior Sister, I had the worry that I'd never get to the missions, and I made a pact with the saint. "If you get me to Japan, I will go up Mount Hiei and tell at least one monk your truth." I realized that I was not alone. In *The Seven Storey Mountain*, Merton describes the "pact" he made with his patron saint, Therese of Lisieux. "If I get into the monastery," he bartered, "I will be your monk." I thought I could hack the life of a missioner in Japan even if my juggling skills were nil.

So, during my daily walk for the two years at language school in Kyoto, I kept an eye on the mountain and said I would keep my promise. At last, one day all arrangements had been made, and I went up Mount Hiei with a friend to meet the custodian of one of its most beautiful temples, Shakado. The monk's name was Horisawa Somon.

I was still in our traditional long black habit. He was at a low table, placed over a warm *hibachi* (a container for burning coals), around which he had placed two other sets of cushions. He motioned my friend and I to seat ourselves. Putting his hands on his thighs, he bowed deeply and slowly, and then without a word, made a cup of green tea. His movements were flowing and arresting, and performed in utter silence. He bowed solemnly again; my friend and I endeavored to emulate and followed his lead in drinking the tea. Gone was the silence. Instead, there was loud, appreciative slurping. *That* we did not try to emulate!

At the end of the second cup of tea, the monk turned to me and asked, "How do you pray?" (Now, nearly 40 years

37

later, we are still on the same subject.) When I asked what he meant, he replied, "Well, for instance, what about your body position?" I hastily assured him that body position is not important in prayer, and he heartily disagreed. "Body position is *very* important in prayer."

When we seekers go to the East to dip into its fount of wisdom, we are soon confronted with the fact that the body *is* important for all of life. This is becoming evident all over the world, especially in First World countries, where weight and form have taken on a cult of their own. But I should have intuited body participation in prayer on my own. My brother, Bill, was researching the family ancestry, and I consequently formed a strong rapport with the Scottish roots he unearthed.

The old Celtic wisdom, which is enjoying a new springtime of life these days, speaks of the body as our home. Its sages sing of the human body as clay, finding a form and shape that it never found before. In this individuality, inner impulses surface for expression and light, and beg to be brought to voice. Stopping for a moment on the walls of a castle on the Isle of Skye, I read of an anthropologist (MacInnes by name) who a hundred years ago said that the old Celtic sages sang of joy and sorrow which arose from their memories and that in each of us part of the unknown mystery of life becomes luminous. The descendants of the ancient Celts still inhabit the world, still singing and writing poetry of joy and sorrow, rooted in the body as home.

I don't find much of a parallel between this expression of Celtic wisdom and Oriental insights which respect the body, but there was an experience which made it real for me. One afternoon in the Quezon City Convent of the Good Shepherd Sisters in the Philippines, I was having tea with a young Korean sister, and suddenly the building began to shake violently. Since we were on the lowest floor, I grabbed her arm and pulled her out of doors. The gardener was stretched out on the earth, away from the building. He hollered for us to do the same. As I lay there eye level with the heaving wet earth, I suddenly saw earth and I are not two. In the joy of that revelation, I cried out, "I AM THE EARTH!"

On reflection afterward, I recalled how many of the mystics of the great religions came to sing this same song. Rumi, the great Sufi poet, writes:

I am the mote from the sun
I am the sun's circuit
to the mote I say, Hither!
And to the sun I say, Hence!

I am the glimmer of dawn,
I am the air of eventide;
I am the rustling of the branch
The roar of the sea.

I am the bird-catcher, bird and net
I am the face and mirror, voice, and its branches;
I am silence and thought, tongue and talking.

I am the breath of the flute,
I am the spirit of humans;
I am the spark from the stone,
The sheen of metals.

I am war and peace, battlefield and victory;
the town and its besiegers,
the stormers and the wall.

I am hart and lion, lamb and wolf;
I am the shepherd who gathers all into one fold.

I am the chain of being;
I am the ring of the worlds
The ladder of creation, mounting and fall

I am what is and is not,
I am . . . you who KNOW, say it . . .
I am the soul in the ALL.

The sacredness of the body is indeed well known to mystics. Especially in all Oriental disciplines, the teachings support and give rise to that insight. I'd like to outline the way it is taught in Zen. But first I'd better say something about Zen itself, especially as it was introduced to me that day on the top of Mount Hiei. What is Zen? Where did the name come from? What does it mean? And what might this practice say to a Christian?

Zen as known today comes to us through the Buddhist religion. Buddhism was born in India, but its roots extend back to the 17th century BCE, when Aryans from what is now Iran invaded the Indus Valley in central India and subdued the indigenous population. They imposed their religious ideas, which are found in a collection of odes known as the Rig-Veda. In her interesting book *A History of God,* British author Karen Armstrong outlines the belief, at that time, of the existence of a multitude of gods, presenting the forces of nature as instinct, with power, life and personality. There were also signs that people were beginning to see that the various gods might simply be manifestations of one divine Absolute that transcended them all. The Aryans were aware that their myths were not factual accounts of reality, but expressed a mystery that not even the gods themselves could explain adequately. In their travels eastward, the Aryans found the Vedic culture in India well developed, and melding their own insights within it, founded a religion and culture of high renown contained in what are called the Dravidic books. They were written between the years 3000 and 1500 BCE. There we can find the word *dhyana,* which translates as "meditation." Also, some of the artifacts of that period represent a meditator in the lotus position, so right from its very roots, body position seems to have been decided.

By the eighth century BCE, changes in the social and economic conditions of the Indian subcontinent meant that the old Vedic religion was no longer relevant, because it had become preoccupied with the rituals of sacrifice. However, a revived interest in the old Indian practice of yoga (the yoking of the powers of the mind by concentration) meant that religions which concentrated on externals became unpopular. People wanted to discover the inner meaning of these rites. In other words, men and women of that time and place sought to achieve an inward realization of truth. The gods had lost their importance and preeminence. Henceforth, they would be superseded by the religious teacher. Armstrong says that this remarkable assertion of the value of humanity and the desire to take control of destiny would be the great religious insight of the subcontinent.

I can't help but wonder if this very reality is not happening again today.

In any case, reason was not denied, but transcended. The experience of transcendence could not be explained any more than a piece of music or poem can be. The ideal of personal transcendence was embodied in the yogi, who would leave his family and abandon all social ties and responsibilities to seek enlightenment, which gave an insight into another realm of being. About 538 BCE, a young prince, Siddhartha Gautama, became obsessed with the mystery of pain. He left his kingdom and wife and child, to find the reason for suffering. He became a mendicant ascetic and for about six years sat at the feet of several *gurus* and underwent fearful penances. These brought him only fatigue and despair. After a dream, he accepted food, which renewed his vigor and gave him insight that a middle path was to be preferred. He henceforth devoted himself to meditation, and eventually came to an experience.

The name "Buddha" refers to an awakened person. A Buddha is a person who is awakened to his or her very nature. This is an experience of the marriage of transcendence and the self. It cannot be explained or given to another. To live one's life in harmony with this truth brought new hope of liberation and the attainment of *nirvana* (emancipation) for all. Gautama had become the Buddha, the Awakened One. He spent the next 40 years tramping around India, teaching.

Gautama apparently did not want to start a religion. He taught his followers that they should come to realization themselves, and then live their life of right living by what they had experienced. He never thought he had discovered something new. He taught his disciples about what they already possessed and only had to be experienced. He is reported to have said, "I have seen an ancient Path, an ancient Road, trodden by Buddhas of a bygone age." It had objective reality, not because it could be demonstrated by logical proof, but because anyone who seriously tried it found that it worked. But he allowed none of this teaching to be recorded. After his death, his followers began to recount what they remembered, and gradually his followers lived by those sayings instead of their own experience. So Buddhism became a religion – indeed, one of the greatest missionary religions of all times – and its experience of transcendence has generally accompanied the external practices and journeys, although usually somewhat belatedly.

Buddhism as a religion came to China about the same time as the birth of Christ. Zen meditation came as its core about four centuries later. The first Zen missioner, known as Bodhidharma, is perhaps more mythical than real, and the work of establishing Zen in China from India was undoubtedly the result of the work of many people. The exact dates remain unknown. The Chinese made no attempt to change the sound of the Sanskrit word *dhyana* (meditation), but their efforts at pronouncing it resulted in something that sounded like *channa,* which was shortened to *chan.* The ideogram they chose to symbolize the word in their language is a combination of the characters for "infinite" and "simple" with the intimation of "offering." Thus we have some idea of the scope of early Chinese Buddhism religion. It was a simple (not complex) offering with and to the Infinite.

As to the meditation leading to the experience which was the core of the religion, quiet sitting was used, a tradition they probably received from India. There is ample documentation that the teachers in India revered silence, although the enlightenment experience is often portrayed there as having 52 steps. This changed somewhat when Zen met Chinese Taoism, whose meditative experience could be instantaneous just as the Buddha experienced. Zen as we know it today is usually said to have come to us from China.

The Way of Zen silences the body and mind by means of a specific posture and breath absorption while we sit on the *zafu* (a small, round cushion) in what the Buddhists call "awareness of being" in our daily lives. Zen as a discipline acts therapeutically, and builds up *joriki* (a settling power), which leads eventually to a specific religious experience. History teaches us that as a result of having that experience, Zen monks were inspired to perform external expressions of compassion. Zen is not and has never been self-indulgent navel-gazing!

In the seventh century CE, a Korean emperor sent to the Japanese Emperor to whom he felt indebted the gift of some Buddhist priests. The Japanese soon became enamoured not only of the religion, but also of the fact that the monks could make marks on papyrus that they could later read. In other words, the Japanese had not as yet a written language, and the Chinese Buddhists had. In any case, the Japanese very soon were going to the fountain and source of these two attributes to study. Their effort to pronounce Channa or Chan sounded like Zenna or Zen. And of course it is a historical fact that Japanese characters for writing are derived from Chinese.

That day on Mount Hiei, Horisawa San taught us what *zazen* is and how to do it. With the first syllable *za*, "to sit on the floor," we started orientation with the teaching of what to do with the body to help us come to silence and then to experience. Generally speaking, for sitting we follow the age-old practice of yoga, which is to assume a stable, balanced posture, a straight spine, and the breath moving in and out of the lungs freely. However, there are some ways in which we in Zen differ from yogic sitting. Primarily we use two cushions: the *zabuton*, a large, square cushion which acts as a buffer for the knees and ankles, and the *zafu*, a small, round cushion which rests atop the *zabuton* and lifts and supports the spine. Both cushions are well-stuffed with kapok, as they need to be firm.

It is best to wear clean and comfortable baggy clothing, so as not to constrict blood vessels that supply the muscles with much-needed oxygen and nourishment. We were told to sit the way we can. There are six positions available so we were able to find some relief when one particular stance became painful.

Contrary to popular humor epitomized by the remark "Don't do something, just sit there!" Zen is neither punishment nor asceticism. It is well situated within the area of discipline, so we just do the possible. It is also advisable to exercise the body appropriately. There are particular exercises for particular points, most importantly to loosen the groin. Depending on age and other such factors, we gradually become proficient in several positions, including the Full Lotus. Horisawa San stood on his head for 15 minutes that day to illustrate something or other. Later I was to find enormous help from simply soaking in an *ofuru* (honorable bath).

The main fact seems to be that we are to establish three points of body contact with the *zabuton* (the large, square cushion to support the ankles and knees). Usually these are the two knees and the buttocks. They must form a solid tripod. If we cannot make the contact points, then we insert a small auxiliary cushion to fill in the space between the knee and the floor. These three points need a lot of support, otherwise the body will be wobbly. Dogen Zenji, the founder of Soto Zen in Japan, said that we must "sit like a mountain." A mountain is a solid mass and has a good broad base.

In sitting, the central part of the body is of course the back, which must receive special attention. The normal curve of the spine is retained. In the *dojo* (the place of practice), the people monitoring are constantly correcting back positions. What we do with the spine in sitting is of utmost importance. Good posture helps our *zazen*. The popular Indian Jesuit the late Anthony de Mello used to say that slouching brings distractions. A bad sitting posture can also contribute to spinal distress, one of the world's most common physical complaints today. It has been said that our spinal column was originally designed so that we could swing gracefully in trees. That is a long way from sitting upright on cushions, sedentary for many hours. Doctors tell us that lack of exercise, bad posture and obesity are the most prevalent causes of back trouble, and they advocate daily exercise, weight loss and posture correction, as well as a firm mattress and bedboard for sleeping.

For daily living today, exercise is indispensable, and we applaud the current physical fitness enthusiasm with its emphasis on conditioning, proper weight and a healthy diet. There are many excellent exercise programs to be found. Being in the field of Oriental spirituality, we tend to stress yoga or one of the variations of T'ai Chi. When seekers come to me with some kind of program in mind, I underline the fact that it must include the whole body and must also be in harmony with the psyche and Spirit. The movements are to be done with breath awareness. With correct posture and proper cushions, the blood vessels are free to bring oxygen and nourishment to the muscles and carry off wastes. Lower back pain is a warning that something is wrong; do not disregard it.

Horisawa San taught us the six available positions:

Full Lotus: Seat yourself on the front third of the *zafu,* the small, round cushion. Put the right foot on the left thigh and the left foot on the right thigh. Draw the heels up to the abdomen, but leave the toes free to wiggle. This position is the most difficult, but also the best because there is the least distortion to the spine. It is obviously the most symmetrical.

Half-Lotus: Tuck the right foot under the left thigh and place the left foot on top of the right thigh. This position is the one most used by the majority of sitters. It is only partially symmetrical. Compensate for this by adjusting the round zafu under your torso, until the spine is as upright as possible. You may also put the left foot under the right thigh, and the right foot on top of the left thigh. This position may require a slightly higher *zafu.*

Burmese: Draw the right foot up close to the left thigh or vice versa, allowing the foot, calf and knee to rest on the *zabuton.* Then place the left leg in front of the right, so that both knees touch the cushion. This requires a still higher *zafu.* Adjust positioning of the body carefully, paying particular attention to the spine.

Kneeler: Tuck a kneeler under the thighs and sit on it. A kneeler is a small wooden bench and can be used to relieve a lot of the leg pressure in sitting. A thin cushion on top of the kneeler is helpful.

Seiza: With knees apart, put a high, thick *zafu* between the heels. Lower the buttocks well over the *zafu.* Adjust the hips until comfortably seated. This is a position often used in Japan for ordinary quiet sitting.

Chair: Beginners are generally reluctant to use a chair for sitting. It may, however, be the only way to sit temporarily until you get in shape for floor sitting. For older people with permanent disabilities, it may be the only position. A flat stool or unupholstered chair is preferable. Place a *zafu* on the seat and sit on the front third as directed above. The feet are flat on the floor, shoulder-width apart; the legs of the chair should be adjusted so that the knees are slightly lower than the hips. Straighten the spine and do not lean against the back of the chair. An adjustable piano stool would be ideal.

Mudra (hand position): While sitting in *zazen*, the hand position has always been considered to be of utmost importance, and is called the *mudra*. *Mudra* is a Sanskrit word which means "seal," and refers to physical gestures, especially hand movements, which are meant to evoke certain states of mind. In the *zazen mudra*, the hands are still, the right hand resting palm up on the sitter's lap, the left hand placed on top of the right hand, and the two thumb tips touching lightly, so that the hands form an oval shape. They are then drawn toward the navel. The actual placement of the hands will vary according to the leg position used. For instance, in the full lotus, the hands will rest on the heels. In all positions, let the arms relax as much as possible.

Many people feel comfortable with their hands on their knees, but Zen insists on the *mudra*. Several Japanese acupuncturists went to study in China after it opened its doors to the world. They returned home exclaiming they now understood why Zen sitters use the *mudra*, for it connects energy cycles that course through the meridians of the body.

The eyes are lowered to a spot on the floor about one meter directly in front of the nose. They are open and seeing, but not looking, and resting on the spot. They will not necessarily remain in focus. The mouth is closed, but the teeth are not biting, and the tip of the tongue is resting against the upper front teeth. This helps prevent over-salivating.

Perhaps the last word on keeping the body in harmony with our other dimensions has been said by Raimon Panikkar: "Once I begin to understand the body, I am humble. We have to undergo the process of incarnation identifying our daily selves with our body. This process demands asceticism, not because of fear of sinfulness, but because without asceticism, we lose freedom."

Much of this I heard about Zen from Horisawa San on the top of Mount Hiei. Suddenly, that March afternoon seemed to get dark. The young monk looked at his watch and apologetically reminded us that the last funicular would be returning to Kyoto in 10 minutes. I gasped that I had not told him about the great Christian missioner who had tried to come up Mount Hiei some centuries before. "You mean Francis Xavier," Horisawa San smiled. "I know all about him. We weren't very nice to him. I'll try to be nicer to you."

Thus on March 25, 1963, did I keep my promise to the great Jesuit missioner, gain a foothold on the ladder of Oriental spirituality, and find a lifelong friend in this now famous Tendai Buddhist monk, Horisawa Somon.

Chapter Four

Becoming Free through Self-Knowledge

The stream of Zen to which I belong is headed at the moment by Kubota Ji-un Roshi. A couple of years ago, he attended the graduation of his son at Harvard University. At the ceremony, the valedictorian spoke of her search for knowledge. "I came to this university with two questions: Who am I? and Why am I here? I am graduating with a Doctor of Philosophy degree seven years later, and I still do not know the answer to either of those questions." Kubota Roshi told me later that it was all he could do not to rush to her and explain that those questions can be answered. To ponder them is, for the Oriental, part of the human condition. These days, the questions seem to be universal.

The best-selling book *Sophie's World* deals almost exclusively with who-am-I and why-am-I-here questions, and is a startling revelation of present-day interest in philosophy. Thirty-five years ago, whenever English-speaking seekers visited Kamakura and asked to speak with Yamada Roshi, I sometimes interpreted for them. When the Roshi asked why they had come such a great distance, they would invariably reply, "I want to find out who I am."

Finding out who we are, as individuals, and in my case as a member of a religious order, is an ongoing journey. I recall that in one of the convent readings included in our daily Office, all Christians are told why they are here. In her book *New Wineskins,* Sandra Schneiders expresses it this way: "Our activity is . . . co-operating with the Creator God in transforming history into God's reign of justice and love." This is, of course, based on the belief that we are children of God. In any case, many people believe they are in this world to help in its transformation. So what are they questioning? Maybe they are really saying, "There is a part of me that I don't understand, and I am restless until I find out what that is and experience it myself."

My old Jesuit friend the late Fr. Enomiya Lassalle used to warn that the problem in the late 20th century was that we live too much in our heads. In Christian meditation we pray in our head and with our heart. We create an object. We can *imagine* an entry into the spiritual world, but what we image is an object, and therefore creates a two, which is a mis-representation of the spiritual world. And also it will be of our making, which is fine for relational prayer. A human being is a relational person, and to utter the supreme statement *I love you* presupposes two. That is why I do Christian meditation every day, and encourage my Christian disciples and inquirers to do likewise. This type of prayer is not unknown in the Orient. *Bakhti* means devotional prayer, and keeps the fires of love burning in our heart. But a real gut experience tells us that we and our ideal in the spiritual world are *not* two. A true experience in faith will tell us this also, because it is a basic truth. But to know it through faith and to know it through experience are not the same thing. As my colleague and mentor

Ruben Habito is fond of saying, we may have knowledge about electricity, but to touch a live wire is something else!

There is, I think, another problem which confuses most of us today. It is the unclear use of the words "spirit," "spiritual" and "spirituality." Especially the latter term, spirituality, is used so indiscriminately that it risks losing all specific meaning. Sandra Schneiders gives a definition: "Spirituality is the experience of conscious involvement in the project of life integration through self-transcendence towards the ultimate value one perceives" ("Mapping the Terrain," *Theological Education Magazine*, Lent 1999). This definition is broad enough to involve both religious and nonreligious spiritualities, and specific enough that it does not include virtually anything that anyone espouses.

Spirituality is an experience, a lived reality, not a theory or a movement or an abstract idea. As said in the Orient, it involves one's whole life: body, mind and spirit. A high from a double scotch is not an experience in spirituality. Spirituality is a consistent self-transcendence toward the ultimate. But this is a kind of theoretical understanding. Insights from my Oriental meditational practice lead me to agree with the Canadian Catholic priest and author Ronald Rolheiser, who reminds me that spirituality is what I do with the fires that burn within. This articulation puts me into the verb world, where I am more at home.

I still find it helpful to distinguish between spiritual and mystical. The former is the practice, the latter is the experience. The ultimate in the spiritual life can be mistaken and tragic, as we see in some of the cults of our day. So, spirituality requires discernment. But the ultimate in the world's great religions as found in their mysticisms has been proclaimed by all serious practitioners and scholars as the one divine Absolute. True mystics all over the world and all through time have agreed.

Only when people have developed the capacity to transcend the self (or, as I would prefer to say, open the self to be transcended) to a remarkable degree do we regard people as "saints" or as people of remarkable spirituality. The adjective "spiritual" derives from St. Paul who coined it to denote that which is influenced by the Holy Spirit. The basis is therefore religious and positive and en-lifeing. But "spirituality" has, in the last few decades, become a generic term for the life-ing of the human capacity for self-transcendence.

Another baffling use of the word today is in the sense of merely nonmaterial and identified with energy. I have heard the *Roshi* vigorously object to this hypothesis, saying that Buddha Nature is more than energy. I was recently confronted by a yoga teacher who claimed to be an agnostic, not believing in the sacred, but nevertheless very spiritual. Knowing what I do about the Source of Oriental disciplines, I responded that from the yoga standpoint, which is firmly based in the one divine Absolute, that statement is impossible. Everything said in this book is an effort to underline the Sacred in the spiritual.

But I do not for a moment want to suggest that Oriental spirituality can be completely understood. The life-integration which finally leads to an experience of the one divine Absolute defies words. In fact, it is almost useless to say anything, and yet we continue to write books about IT! At some point, our life-integration should speak to the repining restlessness within and be an incentive to practice the way to experience the Sacred. The experience covered in the Sanskrit word *advaita* (not two) is not different from the experience of the Japanese word *satori*. People who have not had the experience usually say it is a realization of oneness, because that is understandable and not wrong. We all get this feeling during moments of high perception. But oneness usually points to some-thing, often something we can see. In the true, clear experience, there is nothing or, better still, no-thing to see. So how can it be truly called "one"? Yamada Roshi used to say, "It is not even one." Therefore, it is true to say "not two," which denies objectivity. That is the deep truth in a mystical experience. Our Christian mystics agree. Eckhart says we can only know God by what God is not.

For the Buddhist, a deep *satori* is synonymous with salvation or certainly a large step toward the other shore. Buddhists call IT their own inherent Buddha Nature, or the empty-Infinite as Yamada Roshi used to say. When we touch that inner Nature, or inner Essence, or whatever tag we want to use, we sink into that sea of Essence or Infinity, which opens us to the Reality that we and the Infinite are not-two. We come to understand that not only are we not-two, we are not even one. "One" is an entity, with a boundary, so to speak. The experience is beyond boundary. At that moment, all boundaries are gone.

There is still another concept which misappropriates the *advaita* experience. As said previously, any number of times I hear people say, "I have found my true self." Or "I never knew I had a true self until my meditation teacher told me and I have now found my true self." It sounds like finding something. No true mystics would endorse that articulation. There is a Zen saying, "The joy of the raindrop is to enter the ocean." When a raindrop sheds its boundary and enters the ocean, there are no boundaries anywhere. The raindrop doesn't find its true self. The raindrop is gone. There is only the ocean. The raindrop becomes nothing, as it were.

I cannot convey it in words, and frequent use of the word "nothing" tends to suggest ennui or boredom. But in reality, the *advaita* experience is one of great joy.

Of course, it stands to reason that the experience has to be confirmed. And by someone who KNOWS. How could anyone confirm themselves? I had had several experiences as my state of consciousness was deepening. And when the inner knot broke open that December night in Kamakura, I had to go to the *Roshi* to be examined and be told it had been a *kensho* (*ken,* to see, and *sho,* our nature) experience. The insight was quite different from anything I had ever experienced before. Although I suspected it might be a *kensho,* I did not know. Of course I later identified it as an experience of union, but when I sat before the *Roshi* to be examined I never even considered that articulation. I related what happened to me. I had disappeared. Body fell away. Everyday consciousness fell away. When that happens, the disciple perceives in a different and unique way, and later, responds to certain questions in a different way. And it is on the evidence of those responses that the *Roshi* begins to consider whether or not there was a true *satori* (enlightenment) experience.

After a deep and confirmed experience, no meditator could possibly say, "I am an agnostic." That is tantamount to saying in the above-mentioned example that "there is no ocean." The meditation that leads to this insight is Oriental Silent Meditation, which *does* tell us who we are. It is a moment of great joy. Buddhists say the greatest vicissitude of life is the problem of life and death. The *advaita/kensho* experience sheds some light on that problem and brings a measure of peace.

Well, so who are we? We have looked at our mystical side. Now let us consider the phenomenal. Phenomenally, we are unique. Zen says we are born free, but very soon develop certain personality traits that are shaped or caused by our environment. When my two sisters and I were cleaning out our family home shortly after our mother's death, we came across many of her little treasures. One of these was my Baby Book. There I discovered that I had been baptized by water from the Jordan River. And there were other tidbits of information such as, "Baby can be bribed for almost anything if fish for dinner is the promise."

Then there was a whole paragraph beginning: "Baby likes to eat out." This was interpreted as exhibiting a potential toward being an epicurean, a certain independence and proclivity toward self decision-making, illustrated by demanding my own menu from a highchair perch. Apparently I would pretend to read the menu, even though it was, more often than not, upside down. Eventually I would give it to my father (my mother noted I didn't seem to trust her), and ask him to read it to me. After a considerable period of reflection, I would order what I wanted. It was often different from the family choices.

At that time, I couldn't have been more than two or three years old. The baby is now in the midst of old age, and still likes to eat out. I continue to read the whole menu first. If fish is listed, I most frequently choose that, and despite many years in Japan, where all the members of a dining party are culturally conditioned to order the same food, I have no shyness if my menu choice differs from the choice of others. As well, I am free enough to order identical sushi with Japanese friends. It doesn't take long for my dining companions to reveal their feelings about this. If they are comfortable with my decision, then there is the tiniest nod of consent. We all settle into the food without comment, except for the rather loud noises of appreciation. Fortissimo!

But I was not culturally conditioned to eat noisily. I recall a *sesshin* (Zen retreat) with the Buddhist nuns at Enkoji. We were having noodles for the evening meal, which were served unadorned on top of a thick pancake of dark *miso* (fermented bean paste), which tended to be so strong and bitter that I used to call it *samurai miso*. The noise was unbelievable as the 12 or so nuns slurped a pile of coated noodles into their mouth with chopsticks. I was looking around for sugar to make the *miso* palatable, and wishing for the absence of a front tooth to provide an easy slurp, but was unable to come up with either advantage. Suddenly, the nun next to me announced in a booming voice, "MacInnes San should show appreciation for the food by making noises" or something to that effect in Japanese. It is not easy to convey one single strand of cold sticky noodle from plate to gullet with the approved audible accompaniment!

Our Western culture, anyone's culture, does not give us the freedom to be our true deep selves. To be truly one's self. What a gift! And how necessary for satisfactory and effective interrelationships. It presupposes that we have sorted ourselves out to a satisfactory degree, and it also presupposes that our companions have as well. They have to be able to let us be ourselves. That is the problem in relating. Especially in the field of spiritual direction, the director has to be a free person. In his first letter to the Corinthians, Paul speaks of his spirituality and finding the new self, which gives him perfect freedom. He was able to say, "I made myself all things to all men" (9:22). Zen sees this possibility coming only through freedom. Zen would also have some difficulty in accepting the authenticity of the popular Christian title "a wounded healer." His strict insistence on the authenticity of the Zen experience for his teachers caused Yamada Roshi often to quip, "You can't give what you haven't got!"

Another interesting point for me on this topic is acting. Jeremy Irons is one of the patrons of the Prison Phoenix Trust, an organization founded to teach meditation in prisons. We asked him to help out at a fundraising event, an evening of readings with his wife, Sinéad Cusack, at Grendon Prison, just outside Oxford. I found myself sitting in the front row for the performance, seeing acting as never before. Sinéad acted beautifully and received a thunderous applause. But Jeremy didn't appear to act at all. For his performance that night, he *was* Tony the lifer at HM Prison Kingston; he *was* the Man of Everest, Sherpa Tenzing. He *was* the seven-year-old brother of Sammy who wees right through someone's mailbox. He *was*

Richard II in all his royal failure! Jeremy admitted this to me later. Even though I had heretofore thought of famous actors as having large egos, I found myself remarking to this interesting man that he must be sure to be Jeremy Irons offstage.

Since we so often have to use different aspects of our personality in relationships and interactions with others, it is important that we know who we are both mystically and psychologically. It is not healthy to lose our identity. And we have to live with ourselves as well as with others. Which is perhaps why psychology is enjoying its preeminence today. It purports to help us come to know who we are at a psychological level.

In our journey toward this discovery, most of us own a self-ignorance and a certain inner restlessness. I have found to be very helpful one system of self-discovery, a system which reaches back into the distant past and whose history has yet to be discovered authentically. Although now frequently presented devoid of any religious significance in the hands of psychologists, it apparently evolved from a mystical and religious basis. It is called the Enneagram.

Ennea is the Greek for "nine," and *grammos* is "figure." A geometric figure is its heart, and it came from the universal insight that human beings are spiritual presences, that they are incarnated in the material world, and embody the same spirit of the one divine Absolute. The Enneagram recognizes the external differences in appearance, which are designated by the same term as Zen: these external differences are only veils of illusion, and beneath or behind these illusions is the Ultimate Source of Be-ing.

It is said that the Enneagram began as a search for a program of human transformation, and has been used through the centuries by people of virtually all religions. It has been able to do this by concentrating on human externals and not doctrinal differences. In certain cases, I have found it complements the slow Zen transformation process for many of my disciples. It certainly helped me as I proceeded to steer this epicurean-gifted self into the subtleties of mystical prayer.

It is very difficult to find a written history of the origin of the geometric figure of the Enneagram. In Don Riso's fine book, *The Wisdom of the Enneagram*, we find one explanation that it was first conceived as a symbol, and is known to have existed in Babylon about 2500 BCE. It contained three elements: the circle, the triangle and the hexad. Put together, they made a symbol in three parts representing the Three Divine laws that govern all of existence. But here all the explanations that I have studied seem to break down. Perhaps only the circle remains unassailable, for it is a universal mandala (circle, assemblage, picture) used in almost every culture in the world. It is certainly most prominent in Celtic art and is the identifying feature of a Celtic cross. The circle refers to unity, wholeness and oneness. It symbolizes that God is one, the distinguishing feature of the major Semitic religions: Judaism, Christianity and Islam. The Greeks saw the circle as the most perfect motion, because it was perpetually turning and returning to its original point; the circling celestial spheres imitate the divine world as best they can.

For certain reasons, not all of which I can satisfactorily explain, the circle seems to find expression in my body during meditation. When I sit in the prescribed Zen (yogic) way, I am conscious of a circle, more or less perfected by my encircling arms. The body meridians seem to conduct the life force in this circular motion.

And I wonder about the source of Eckhart's insight: "All created things are in God's circle so that they may flow out and return." To which he added, "Being is God's circle." The circle is rooted in the spiritual world, but to give the same spiritual prominence to the triangle and hexad is not so evident.

In any case, put together, the circle, triangle and hexad form the symbol of the Enneagram. In some inexplicable manner, the nine personality types which come from the ancient tradition of the nine Divine Attributes reflected in human beings were fitted into the meeting points of the triangle and hexad on the circle's perimeter. It was apparently used in a religious brotherhood that lived in community in Russia early in the second millennium. The Sufis of a later era used and refined it in their spiritual direction.

In working with this system of identification, we own our shadow side, the defenses we have built up, which were determined by our early life situation. Our defenses are a subtle kind of wall-building which make us feel separate and different. By "working on" these indicators, one can climb the ladder of transformation and become more open and free.

When reading my Baby Book, I could see that I started to develop characteristics of a certain type at an early age. Without knowing anything about a type Seven personality, I eventually was able to identify with some of its other characteristics: an adventurer, a multi-tasker, a wunderkind, a dilettante, a connoisseur. Most charts agree that a number Seven would never be found on a Zen retreat. That shows my ornery side!

Unfortunately, even though there seems to have been a sincere effort to maintain its sacred and esoteric message, in reality, it was only a matter of time before the Enneagram left the hands of retreat masters and became a tool for psychologists. In these hands, it seems devoid of its Sacred foundation, and now becomes merely a professional tool. Today, there is some caution expressed in the Church about the Enneagram. There are those who say that the religious element doesn't matter. But it has been my experience, as in the case of the yoga teacher

I mentioned earlier, that the exclusion of the Sacred usually feeds into a block of prejudice. That poison creates boundaries, and connections (spirituality at work) become blocked.

I have had many difficulties with psychology in my lifetime. I went to it for help, because I often felt myself to be a bomb filled with unused – and dare I say unfused – potential! But I received little or no help from psychology despite the fact that from the 1950s to the end of the 20th century, thousands of people sought solace and cures there. I simply could not believe a lot of Freud's writings. Jung was much more attractive, but I felt his forays into Zen were suspect. I simply don't know how a superficial knowledge of Zen could be an authentic and lasting influence for a specialist of Jung's stature. To my knowledge he was never a serious and consistent sitter, let alone a realized one.

At a weekend retreat in Guelph, Ontario, while participating in a session entitled "Emotional Maturity," I asked what the group leaders meant by their frequent use of the word "psyche." It seems they had not been asked that question before. At the end of the retreat, one of them, a Benedictine nun, spoke to me privately and simply admitted that psychology is a new science and sometimes its supposed findings are turned upside down within a 20-year period.

When I finally stumbled across the Enneagram armed with the information of the restaurant-loving young child who was nevertheless very head-centered, it was no surprise to realize I had evolved as a number Seven. It confirmed the way I found myself psychologically, and I felt affirmed and confirmed in my efforts to attain wholeness and become free. The Enneagram describes a number Seven not as a glutton, but as a person pursuing a variety of positive and stimulating ideas and actions in an attempt to fill up a perceived inner emptiness and enthusiastic drives. I'm okay this way. I celebrate life with the goodness of God-given gifts, friendship and music and books and food and sports and travel and seafood and other delights. Because of these proclivities, I have to engage in regular discipline, otherwise I am not free. And almost everything has to make sense or it is put on the back burner.

Krishnamurti says: "It seems to me that before we set out on a journey to find reality, to find God, before we can act, before we can have any relationship with another, it is essential that we begin to understand ourselves first." In coming to understand ourselves, our spiritual life, even our relationships and other important issues, we gradually come to see that the type of our personality is a crucial factor. Lao Tsu says: "He who knows others is learned. He who knows himself is wise." Although not directly commenting on the Enneagram, perhaps the mathematician, physicist and religious philosopher Blaise Pascal expressed the potential of this tool best when he wrote: "If people knew themselves, God would heal them."

When I entered the convent in 1953 and started to develop spiritually, I eventually found a Way that led me to a certain identification with the Infinite, but there were many facets of my personality, including the shadow side, that had to be brought into line by what I saw in that experience. The Enneagram helped me to integrate the other characteristics it predicted I might own, a busy, fun-loving, spontaneous and versatile human being.

Best of all, though, was discovering that a number Seven is a head person, since I was trying to own sensuousness with this overpowering necessity to figure things out and to make sense. Common sense for a start. Head people do not suffer lazy intellectualism easily. They also have the propensity in their unhealthy and average state to overuse the intellect. The orientation book written by members of the Los Angeles *Zendo* put it succinctly:

From infancy onwards, we are strongly conditioned and taught to rely almost totally upon discursive logic and rational thought. We are generally discouraged from developing or relying on our innate ability to grasp reality intuitively or directly. Such abilities are labelled unscientific and dismissed as weird or even non-existent. Even when dealing with questions of ultimate reality, we are urged to remain in the modes of thought learned in elementary school classes, and not to entrust ourselves to other ways of knowing reality. It isn't so terrible to think logically and analytically if we are designing a bridge or balancing a check book. That's the best way to think and be. But when you get right down to it, discursive linear thinking is useful for certain kinds of tasks, and for others it is quite useless. Like the hammer or the toothbrush, it is a tool intended for certain kinds of jobs. If you use a hammer to brush your teeth, or a toothbrush to drive nails, you are not likely to meet with success.

Silence is the Oriental answer to this problem. Silence stills the brain and intellect and imagination and memory and feelings. And then, as it were, the Sacred Power within can do its thing. There is no boundary. There is no object. Our place of contact is the breath. And somehow, it is the breath (in Hebrew, *ruah*) which brings the silence to the Infinite and gives Zen its religious connotation.

Raimon Panikkar has given articulation for the Christian. He says, "As the mind becomes silent, the third eye of human consciousness opens, and the words of Jesus on the sound eye giving health to the whole person (Matthew 6:22) is realized in personal experience."

One of the best biblical quotations for introducing the Way of Zen to a Christian is the well-known line from Psalm 46, "Be still and know that I am God." Oriental teachers would have us take the advice literally. Biblical scholars tell us that the Hebrew verb "to know" is *yadah*, which also means "to experience." So even the Christian Bible tells us to be still and we will come to experience God.

If that is so, why is silence non–user-friendly to Westerners, whose basic culture is Christian? Why have we lost the art of silence? It is a rare commodity. Many seekers find it is not as easy as turning down the volume on the television or getting a quick fix from some form of drug. It is a practice in the widest and deepest sense of the word. Many psychiatrists are of the opinion that we wouldn't need any doctors at all if the mind were at rest.

Because an overactive mind is the disease of these times, it is not uncommon for spiritual seekers to have forsaken all and travelled to the ends of the earth to find a true teacher in legitimate transmission. The contemporary seeker will not be kept waiting at the gate for a week to gain admission, as was customary in ancient times, but will be expected to demonstrate a willingness to learn, listening not only to one's teacher and to one's own body, but also indeed to the universe itself, and all the 10,000 things in it.

Beginners in contemplation today are cautioned to:

(1) Allow yourself to be emptied.

(2) Let go, so we will have no fear of emptiness.

(3) Give up our busy-ness, which is often a state of mind/habit.

In today's world, psychologists warn that we often exhaust our mind, a mind already alienated by an illusory fear of separation in egotistical pursuits. Many feel a need to belong. The antidote is living life in a kind of openness and then eventually coming to see that indeed, that which binds the world together is ONE, and we are in and of this Oneness. We are community. There is no separation and things are just as they are. Each season is appropriate. The following poem appears in the 19th *koan* in the *Mumonkan,* Zen's most famous book of *koans*, the title of which was translated by my teacher as *The Gateless Gate.*

> The spring flowers, the moon in autumn,
> The cool breezes of summer, the winter's snow.
> If idle concerns do not cloud the mind
> This is man's happiest season.

Silence is the shaft we descend to the depths of contemplation. Silence is the vehicle which takes us to the innermost center of our being, which is the place for all authentic practice. Ruben Habito, a contemporary Christian Zen teacher, friend and mentor, once identified Zen as "an invitation to experience where God dwells." This echoes the words of Exodus (15:17-18): "In your love you led the people you redeemed; you guided them to your holy dwelling."

Real silence is prayer. The spiritual traditions of both East and West attest to this, although the Western voice has been somewhat blurred for centuries. In the old days we frequently heard the chant "*silentium tibi laus*" – silence is the highest and truest praise of God. That being so, I think Zen will eventually find an appropriate niche in Christianity.

Lao Tzu tells us that silence is the great revelation. What does it tell us? Many things along the way, in daily transformation, and eventually silence reveals the Self; we come to know who we are. In his book *Prayer*, Abishiktananda says something to the effect that to experience the Self is the highest possible attainment for a human being.

There are many ways to meditate. There are several kinds of prayer that teach us to be silent. I frequently hear parish priests in Canada speak about a type of prayer that is more contemplative. Zen does without the "more." It is a type of meditation that is completely silent, and therefore totally contemplative. It is the way of silence par excellence. It is a discipline in which we silence and harmonize body and mind and breath, which acts first of all therapeutically, both on us and on our environment. Eventually, when all things are ready, it effects a specific spiritual experience.

How do we start? Once we are seated appropriately on the *zafu* (the small, round cushion about 10 cm high), we watch the breath come in and out for a few sequences, and then start counting the breaths from one to ten. The inhalations will be the odd number, and the exhalations the even. We breathe in the way that is natural for us, counting only to ten. Higher mathematics requires the use of the intellect and memory! Counting the breaths may sound easy, but in practice it is quite difficult to do just that, without being distracted from the count by stray thoughts, memories, fantasies, etc. Our exhalation is longer than the inhalation, and there is a considerable period of time when we seem to do neither. Eventually we can do without counting. And it may not be appropriate to call breath-counting a mind-training exercise for beginners. For some it will be a lifetime practice.

In our stream of Zen, the Sanbo Kyodan, we sit without moving for a 25-minute period, followed by a 5-minute walking meditation called *kinhin*. We do *kinhin* by fisting the right hand and covering it lightly with the left, keeping the eyes focused on a spot about two meters ahead or on the back of the person in front. We walk at a slow pace, each step firm and balancing, being one with our practice of breath-counting all the while. *Kinhin* is designed solely for flexing muscles and tendons and reactivating sluggish blood vessels.

We are urged to sit regularly every day for at least one-half hour or, better still, one regular sit in the morning and one in the evening. For most of us, that hour after first arising in the morning is by far the best time for *zazen*. Then we have a minimum of thoughts and concepts and feelings. Just our breath. We usually give some form of breath-counting to beginners. Frequently they find it too busy, which means that they should just BE the breath. Not difficult, but not easy. In Zen, this practice is called *shikantaza*, and may indeed be the highest form of sitting possible. One night, while I was watching the news with the Yamadas in their home, pictures were flashed from Iran and the revolution that was brewing there came alive on the television screen. Thousands and thousands of young men were jostling one another on the streets and protesting. The unrest was palpable. "I wish I could go there," the *Roshi* said, "and just sit in *shikantaza*. It would provide the settling power for those people to bring about what changes are needed but in a nonviolent way."

Shikantaza is the Zen word for contemplation. Literally translated it means "just sitting." The meditators just sit and give themselves over completely to the Sacred Power. I like to think that we experience this sacredness that we call IT when we are just BE-ING. For me, contemplation is a prayer/meditation of complete silence, body and mind, where we give over to the Infinite Power within. In Eckhart's words, "We let God be God in us." When we do that, we are letting Be-ing depend on us. Only gradually, when all things are ready, will we come to that happening which, if deep, brings us the peace and light that we seek. In the meantime, we have started on a Way that will soon pay dividends in daily life. We experience our own inner change rather soon.

Another point has to do with moving along the Zen process rather quickly. It is beyond the power of a teacher to ascertain what period of time a beginner will take to experience what Zen has to offer, for the pace differs with each individual. Some advance very quickly, and soon come to a deep state of sitting. At such a time, there are certain phenomena that can be experienced, which may be visual, aural or physical body sensations.

Ultimately, these are of no consequence and are to be ignored, but they nevertheless indicate a degree of the sitter's progress and should be reported to the teacher. They are called *makyo* and are representations from the subconscious. Sitting puts us in touch with areas deep in the psyche. This often results in a flow of tears. There is no cause for alarm, as they are often external manifestations of a healing. That inner Power always acts appropriately. The *Roshi* used to say that setting up (by silence) and releasing that Power brings about the transformation of ourselves and our family, our community and our business, our country and our world. That is contemplative meditation. That is *shikantaza*. That is Zen. Allowing the Prime Mover to work.

Meister Eckhart says that in prayer we must do nothing and let God do everything. Not an easy procedure for half of the world's people, where both culture and religion tend to strengthen the ego. This kind of procedure leads us to believe that everything depends on us.

As I write this book, and whenever I speak about my discipline, I have to stress that I am thus appealing to the intellect, but there is not much in Zen that is intellectual. Real Zen activity happens at another level, and the power to reach that level is usually generated on your cushion. Neither words of instruction nor inspiration, no matter how eloquent, can reach that level. The necessity is silencing the mind.

True Zen cannot be understood intellectually. Zen is not going anywhere or doing anything. One of the most satisfactory definitions of Zen is that it is (just) experiencing fully at all times. It has to be practiced and experienced to be understood. Zen is a process and, although uninteresting, some people do persevere in its practice for years. The fact that the *zendo* is crowded each week is an indication that something is happening to the people sitting. Beginners may come rather soon to the point where they experience feeling better on the days they sit in meditation. The mind will gradually shed its shackles and eventually attain peace, because the discipline melts blocks and helps us let go of attitudes and preconceived ideas. That peace is the beginning of harmony.

Sitting with others is also part of Zen. When people sit together, there is an added something that happens in conjunction with all present. This is by way of warning that it is difficult to sit alone. But almost everyone has to learn to cope with that problem.

We are also warned not to waste time on our cushion. Many of us lead very busy lives, and sitting still for 30 minutes presents a great temptation to catch up with planning. We have to be determined to "just sit" during the time allotted for *zazen*. Actually, we can soon become faithful to this daily practice, and not get bogged down with unanswered questions. The experience will come in its own time. Tears and/or *makyo* should always be reported and then forgotten. They are on no account to be cultivated.

In books concerning the Ways of the Orient, there is a plethora of writings about breathing. Even in Zen, there is sometimes a mistaken notion that we should breathe deeply from the abdomen. Four hundred years ago in Japan, it was a historical expediency for a *zendo* with many sick monks to breathe "below the chest" to contain the coughing.

At our Zen Center, we give very simple instructions for breathing. First of all, we breathe naturally. Most Oriental disciplines begin by being breath-centred, and as we breathe in and out in one-pointed concentration, the breath naturally becomes a little slower and deeper, unconsciously. But if it is unnatural, the tendency is to overaspirate and become dizzy. Then the body starts to wobble. All Dogen Zenji says about breathing is to put the breath gently in the nose.

A few years ago, some former disciples sent a book with the following inscription:

> Every breath is a sign
> Of God's desire
> To do what I am doing.
> Every breath and footfall
> Is a sign of God's purpose for me.
> We plan and let go. Keep breathing.

Another word that is widely used in Oriental disciplines is "practice." In the wide sense, it usually designates the spiritual path on which we pattern our daily life. In a narrower sense, we often hear people say, "Zen is my practice." And in an even more particular sense, teachers frequently ask, "What is your practice in Zen?" implying that there are several "things" one can be doing whilst sitting on the *zafu*.

In giving a practice to beginners during the several weeks of orientation, we concentrate on what could be called mind-training exercises. Most people who come to us for orientation know that in Zen one seems to stop the thinking process, but there is no real comprehension of what that entails. We liken it to contemplation, but since that word does not as yet enjoy a very specific connotation, we find it helpful at this stage to add that John of the Cross also sees contemplation as the cessation of sense and spiritual faculties. Specifically, we endeavor to stop linear thinking, even to avoid entertaining random thoughts, and all such mental activities as feeling, remembering, imagining and planning. In other words, we disengage the psyche from all its busy-ness. For people living in the hub of today's world, this is a shift of gargantuan magnitude.

From then on, a great deal of stick-to-it-iveness is needed. And when all things are ready, we are gifted with a *kensho* that shakes the heavens and astonishes the earth. And so there is a haven for the seeker. There are answers to the eternal questions. They come at a cost. But they are there for the seeking.

Chapter Five

Connections and Reciprocity

Japan is a country of delights for any cultural student. Learning the language, I had to venture over several millennia of sensitivity and form. One day, a Japanese priest came to say Mass at the convent. While serving his breakfast afterwards (it was still in the days when sisters and priests did not eat together) I was asked, "Who arranged the flowers in the chapel?" Immediately sensing a negative critique, I did not reveal the sister's name but inquired why he was interested. "Because whoever did it was very angry." He had made a connection.

Perhaps not many of us are equipped to comment on the mood of artists when they execute their works. In Japan, at least until just recently, a teacher in one of the arts (even the martial arts) could tell whether the disciple was proceeding from ego and muscle, or from the power of the Buddha Nature within.

To my knowledge, the most commonly held opinion about the beginning of *ikebana* (flower arrangement) came from a Chinese monk discharging his temple duties after meditation.

He quickly cut a bunch of fresh flowers in the garden, and jammed them into a vase. Something spoke to him of inappropriateness. He dismantled his first effort, and with the basic facts of heaven and earth and human beings, he endeavored to come in touch with the inner promptings. Then, relating to those facts, he tried arranging the flowers to represent the three points. Today, the art of *ikebana* is highly refined, but several schools still base their creations on that original trinity.

I studied *ikebana* for ten years. The *sensei* (teacher) always chose the flowers. She took a newspaper-wrapped bundle, opened it, turned each stem around as she studied which would be the point of heaven, the point of earth, and the point of the human being. She would cut and trim each stalk to the appropriate length and proportion, insert it judiciously into the *kenzan* (a spiked metal holder) and then provide each point with a companion stem. The final touch was either filling in the required spots or leaving them empty and silent. Every week we would admire the completed masterpiece together, and she would instruct me to take it over to my table, study it, take it apart, and redo it. The *sensei* would later come to inspect and comment. That was the lesson. Ten years of this effort and still I would not be expected to advance to the point where I could choose or cut the flowers, and arrange them for her perusal. The form was set, seemingly forever.

On the positive side, it eventually became very satisfying. At the least, it was an exercise in appropriateness in time. I could only imagine what IT was in timelessness. The statement the flowers made became a profound passageway between the Essential world and the phenomenal world. Eventually, I conceded that the arrangements I did on my own at home usually lacked subtlety. At best the effort often seemed to lack spiritual dimension. I knew there was an ideal in the art of *ikebana*, and that a fine teacher who would have had a *satori* experience could reflect that. Thus the connection between the Absolute and the Absolute working in our world. Flower art is a reciprocity with the Divine. It involves a connection that sensitive and gifted people all over the world can make instinctively. It is my delight that a large number of teachers and "connectors" have proliferated abroad, which speaks volumes for the art's transcendence in various cultures and religions.

Usually in the Japanese/Buddhist arts, there is an economy of means. The most is said with the least. This has been a force of influence for me. Not only in flower arrangements, but in writing and speaking, if I have the option, I prefer to cut out all unnecessary words. As far as *ikebana* is concerned, the teacher will take a branch which is beautiful in form, and she may clip and slice it up until perhaps just one leaf remains. But that leaf speaks volumes!

Another sister was studying with me. One day, the principal stem of the flowers given us vaguely resembled a *bonsai* (an artistically stunted tree), in this case a weeping willow. The small shower of branches was utterly captivating. I held my breath as *sensei* chopped away the various rivulets, but the end result was truly arresting. Then she arranged the other flowers to complete the presentation. We studied it together, and then, as usual, I dismantled it, put it together again, and after the teacher had inspected the effort, took it apart once more. After class, as was my custom, I carried the bundle home. When I looked in our small convent chapel that evening, I was speechless. The other sister studying with me was unable to let the teacher disturb her tree of showers, and there it stood in all its splendor, in a flat ice-blue dish on the chapel floor. *Ikebana* be damned. (I understood her feelings completely!)

During that period, I also tried other Japanese Ways, such as *shodo,* the Way of Calligraphy, and *sado,* the Way of Tea. The encounter with the tea ceremony was unsuccessful but nevertheless interesting. I love the taste of good green tea, which had become a veritable winter comfort during language study in a cold Kyoto building. Our *sado sensei* kept our small class interested as he gave the history of the ceremony which, we were surprised to discover, is not so ancient. The rubrics of the cleansing of the tea cup emulate the movements involved in the cleansing of the chalice at the end of the mass. Francis Xavier, who would have been the first to say mass in Japan, dates his arrival from the end of the 15th century and into the 16th. Tea drinking came from China, where it was first treated as a medicinal herb, but eventually it became a social function around the 19th century. In Japan it was confined for many years to temple use, but with the rise of the samurai, it became the favored pastime of the warring class. Undoubtedly, the ceremony for brewing and serving tea began to be refined in the hands of the artistic Japanese long before that period.

My problem with the *sado* ceremonies came with the size of my body, specifically, when the student has to rise in the graceful, controlled way required in so many of the Japanese arts. The next ritual demands seven steps to the steaming kettle of boiling water. With my long legs, I arrived in a mere two steps and I felt a bit like Gulliver as I tried to shuffle them into seven. Eventually, I reasoned that my path to mysticism might be trod more naturally via another route.

Of course, I also tried Japanese *koto* music. The *koto* is a large, nine-stringed harp which lies on the floor. At first, it seemed extremely easy to play. I could produce the entire melody of *Sakura* by plucking only the open strings! For a time, it didn't seem too difficult to progress to *rokudan* (sixth level). Then I discovered the next step was singing in the Oriental yodelling style! Anyone who has ever heard the strident sounds of a *shamisen* (Japanese lute), which accompanies a nasal, piercing singer in the ancient classical way, will understand why I quickly dismissed the possibility of a Westerner like me making connection with the Infinite with that medium. It didn't take long to grasp the meaning of the Japanese Ways, but how to get the flow going from the art to the great Ultimate Reality proved elusive.

One day in Kamakura, Yamada Roshi twirled a red rose. Then he said, "In its Essential Nature, this is neither red nor a rose." Crash-bang! I got it! I made the connection. In my spiritual journey I had at last moved from intimacy to participation. How? I don't know. It happened in the flash of an eye, and as the saying goes, it was sheer gift. It was not a *kensho* experience but certainly an intuition. Apart from gift, it merely requires no blocks. It's as natural as the flow of water, and as satisfying as water on a hot summer day.

Do I see IT flowing in relation to other people? Yes, and sometimes I feel like a *sensei* (teacher) in one of the Japanese Ways. At such times I seem to know whether the other is acting from ego and muscle or the Source of the Power within. Sometimes when Pete Sampras is playing tennis, I see IT in his movements. Also his "I don't know" reply to a questioning "how?" is neither humility nor ignorance, but something that is consistent with his experience. IT most often is discernible in movement, hence my love affair with verbs. As long as there are no blocks, these are sacred. There are some things which are as they are, to be acceptable as such, and to remain Unknowable.

The Japanese language also mirrors this sensitivity. It is very difficult. For non-Japanese, there is the usual difficulty of mistaking the words themselves. One Maryknoll priest intended to give a sermon on "man" (*ningen*) and instead mistakenly used *ninjin* ("carrot"). The Oriental custom of not showing feelings came to the fore, and there wasn't a smile or snicker from any of the parishioners. The sentence structure in Japanese is based on the cultural surety that feelings are of utmost importance, and to respect this, sentences tend to be long. The verb appears usually at the end of a sentence, with all the descriptive bits first, so that we can take on the feeling of what is to come. This can include the weather and time of day, the mood of place, etc. Later comes the subject, and finally the action. I remember once smiling through the first part of a message, only to discover at the end that the subject had died. I had to dismiss the smile quickly! Hence the benefit of an inscrutable Oriental face!

The ideograms that indicate the words are a monumental obstacle for foreigners, of course. Even more than *kanji* (ideograms) and vocabulary, there is the mountain of sensitivity in the culture itself. Japan is not a classless society. I do not mean this in a derogatory way. It is a society built on each person's uniqueness. There are words used only by and for people whom the culture holds in high respect. Yamada Roshi's position was of the ultimate. We, his disciples, were aware that when cultured Japanese people spoke to him, they used special words and verb forms which we endeavored to emulate. For instance, when I wanted something from a peer, I would use the verb *kudasai*. But when I requested something from Yamada Roshi, I used another verb, *itadaku,* which showed my respect for him, the bestower. I would then put it in the present form of desiring, *itadakitai,* and finally tack on three more words to soften the request, *da to omoimasu* ("I think"). So instead of the one word *kudasai,* when asking something from the *Roshi*, I used *itadakitai da to omoimasu.* Some of the specially gifted foreign students, like my friends Ruben Habito or Larry McGarrell, were talented in language, and having studied under fine teachers, were able to approach the *Roshi* at the appropriate level. But most of us struggled and downgraded the poor man at every turn! To his eternal credit, he almost never showed any displeasure, but I have been sensitive to language ever since.

This presented me with a special difficulty in returning to the West and being confronted with the English language, which can be inaccurate, insensitive, and is probably better suited for scientific representation than human truth and feelings. There are also terms which are not ambiguous for us, but in translation pose an enormous problem. Such terms, especially those used to represent Oriental spiritual realities, have suffered in translation. To give an example, I cite words such as meditation, prayer, ego and mindfulness. Fortunately, they are in use all over the world now, and often it is just as appropriate to use the Japanese word. There is increasing familiarity with words such as *ikebana, Zen, judo, aikido, kendo, dojo,* etc.

Nevertheless, certain words present a unique problem, because the English equivalent is fuzzy in meaning. The word *Zen,* for instance. It is not precisely "meditation" as understood in English terminology, nor is it "prayer" as understood in Japanese. We Christians make no dichotomy between meditation and prayer. Meditation is prayer, although a particular type of prayer. In Japanese, the usual word for prayer is *inoru* and is used for petitions or praise. It is spoken prayer, whether aloud or in the heart. Zen, usually designated as *zazen,* is the well-known discipline of a specified body position, a silent mind, and breath involvement. It is quite different from *inoru* prayer. Most of my colleagues and I use *sitting* as an alternate word, and we tend not to use the word "meditation" for Zen.

There are many discrepancies in the grades of teaching done in the ever-increasing number of *zendos* in North America and the Western world. Much of the negative criticism is accurate. I feel the problems are due in part to ignorance, both in language and substance. As in Oxford, there are at least six *zendos* in Toronto. In how many of these is the leader a qualified Zen teacher? And then there is the baffling (to me) attraction as a religion that Buddhism has for many Westerners. I so often meet people who come to share their enthusiasm for Buddhism, with which I can heartily concur. But usually I am taken aback when some of them profess to be Buddhists. I can understand people realizing they have Buddhist leanings, and perhaps that is what an instant convert is. But admirers of the Catholic Church do not profess to be Catholics until they have undergone the elaborate process of joining the official church.

The Dalai Lama seems to share this hesitation. He has endeavored recently to clear up the issue. For some years His Holiness has been taking a group of American self-made Buddhist monks to Dharamsala, where they live for one month each year. He takes them into teachings beyond the chief tenets of Buddhism, such as The Four Noble Truths and The Eightfold Path, and even further. Accounts of these encounters are extremely interesting. Some of the newly discovered statutes were a complete surprise, some were anticipated, some were rejected. Certainly, when it came to ethical issues about sex, many of the Americans wanted nothing to do with those Buddhist ordinances.

To lay people, the Dalai Lama has counseled that Buddhism, like Christianity, is a religion with its own charter and canons, and to say that Christians can be both Buddhist and Christians, or vice versa, is like putting a sheep's body on a yak's head. Other people feel differently. Many people tell me I am both a Buddhist and a Christian. I understand what they mean, for in its origin, Shakyamuni apparently did not intend to start a religion. From his own experience, he felt that the way forward for human beings was to come to *satori*, find out who they really are, and in the light of what they "saw" in the experience, to live their personal life in interconnection with all creation. We Zen practitioners have no hesitation in claiming that legacy as our own. But in the light of history, can it be said that we are Buddhists?

The problem is that the Buddha's expectations never evolved. Contrary to his wishes, the followers of Shakyamuni started to record his sayings and teachings, and this gave the *sangha* at least a set of canons in which they could profess belief. Thus Buddhism started as a formal religion. Through the centuries, it developed what we would call its own philosophy and theology, became one of the great missionary religions in the world, and produced such delightful, peaceful and religious figures such as our present-day Dalai Lama. Apparently he is understandably worried about the missionary effects of Buddhism today. Even with our almost miraculous methods of instant communication, the Westerners in particular are shaping it to their own preferences.

For our part, Western Zen Buddhist practitioners are clearly rejecting the criticism that Buddhists are navel gazers. All over the world there is a new brand of Buddhist deeply involved in social issues. They are signified by the term Engaged Buddhists. Not long ago, I read of the efforts of British Buddhists to reach out to the dispossessed in society. A recent issue of the magazine *Indra's Network*, produced by a group of Engaged Buddhists in the U.K., includes their mission statement.

> Engaged Buddhism is engagement in caring and service, in social and environmental protest and analysis, in non-violence as a creative way of overcoming conflicts, and in right livelihood and other initiatives which prefigure a society of the future. It also engages with a variety of contemporary concerns of relevance to an evolving Buddhism. Engaged Buddhism combines the cultivation of inner peace with active social compassion in a mutually supportive and enriching practice.

A type of Buddhism is obviously developing in the West, surely the growing points of what Stephen Batchelor, founder and director of the Buddhist College in Devon, calls "a culture of awakening." But Ken Jones, the editor of *Indra's Network,* feels a familiar disquiet about the package. He says,

> In our meditation practice, we learn to open up to whatever discomforts us, and through whole-hearted acceptance, to find an at-oneness. So why do our writings on Buddhist organizations, movements and leaders commonly lack that inclusiveness? Why do we shy away from the shadow side? What becomes of the quest for enlightenment? Has Buddhist activism become so preoccupied with oiling the wheels of radical social change as to lose sight of inconceivable liberation? In other words, does engaged Buddhism need to be freed from the secularizing weight of modernity so that it can become truly a Buddhism of modernity?

I endeavor to take my little message around quietly, that "inconceivable liberation" is the result of the enlightenment experience (*satori*), and suggest putting that into practice. The *satori* experience is the core of Buddhism. Most of the evolving *zendos* in the world today do not treat it as such. As one Korean Zen Master explains it, we are all made of the same cookie dough. If I may transfer the point of inference, I think it is more accurate to refer to the *satori* insight as the leaven and not the dough itself. And to *touch* the leaven is not something henceforth to be referred to as a belief. It is alive and vital. Its work is inter-connecting, totally verb-ish. For the disciple, it is to be practiced. It is practiced by being lived, or to put the accent on the appropriate syllable, it is practiced by be-ing lived. Dare I yet say just "be-ing"? It will involve the disciple in a discipleship of discipline. It is alive and potent and in writing is sometimes most strikingly represented by making verbs out of nouns. I do this by using the "ing" form, for instance, life-ing.

It seems that is the way an Oriental mystic lives. As do some Western saints. A mystic is not an esoteric being beyond the clouds of delusion. A mystic can be a neighbor or even an inmate in prison who has experienced the powerful IT to some degree and been able to faithfully allow IT to take over her or his whole life. Making connections with IT in all of creation. This is why I see Ron Rolheiser's definition of spirituality as indicative of what is going on. As he expresses it, spirituality is what we do with the fires that burn within. Those fires keep the verbs in action. They are a power source. In Christian terms my spirituality is contained in St. Paul's phrase, which I realize I keep returning to throughout this book: "I live now not I but Christ lives within me."

Make no mistake. The inner fires are a source of Power. The well-known Japanese Ways are concerned with the using of this power or, better stated, allowing this power to act. When this is accomplished, the influence of the aggressive ego is cut down to size. Probably not completely obliterated, but at least the aggressive agent is no longer in the driver's seat. *Shodo,* the art of writing Japanese ideographs, is taught first by just doodling, as one holds the brush so that the *IT* power flows easily though arm and hand and brush and ink onto the paper. When this line of action is ascertained by the teacher, the student can proceed to writing the numeral one, which is a short, horizontal isolated line. Three years of doodling without even getting to one made me start to doubt I would ever be a mystic!

Perhaps all this sounds as though disciples in the Japanese arts are being bamboozled into losing their initiative and creativity. But this is not the case. I was not being taught not to use the ego. I was being taught finally to allow St. Paul's phrase into Be-ing. At long last I was bringing "I live the not-I" into daily life, and it has become a kind of mantra for me. Not that

I murmur it ceaselessly. When that be-ing moves into the everyday world in action, as a Christian I call it love-ing.

When I returned to the West after an absence of over 30 years, I found myself studying English words as I had done when I learned Japanese and Cebuano. The word "mindfulness" was especially baffling, for it carries a lot of baggage. I studied its several possible articulations and frequently pondered why that word was chosen to represent the Oriental practice I knew it to be. It certainly doesn't mean to have a full mind. I have endeavored to discover what Westerners mean when they use that word. For many, it means cultivating a good memory. One of Thich Nhat Hanh's followers told me he (the follower) had forgotten his own wife's birthday and therefore his mindfulness was lacking. This suggests to me the word means "the mind is kept full." But that very Buddhist teacher himself defines it as: "to be here . . . to witness deeply in the present moment . . . so that each thought and each action in the sunlight of awareness becomes Sacred."

My own understanding of the term and its practice is more along that line. I think mindfulness means to witness deeply to the present moment, and be open to it. Sometimes I seem to see openness as my practice. I recall being influenced years ago by something Rahner wrote:

> We must be growing always as it were absorbing infinities into ourselves, because it is our business to remain open. And so life, our being, is full of endless potential that we explore only by degrees, step-by-step, piecemeal. If we keep enriching ourselves in this way, accumulating grace and blessings, ever more egoless and faithful, absorbing the Infinite, then we begin to see the kind of love we can give away to others, simply by giving away ourselves.

Mindfulness does have its own meditation, and as *Indra's Network* states, "although its potential is necessarily limited as compared with the ancient path of Buddhist enlightenment, it has the advantage of being accessible to a much wider range of people." Thich Nhat Hanh has become one of the most successful spiritual teachers of our time, and his definition seems both accurate and in the tradition.

Our disciplines are perhaps better served by the word "awareness," although that usually creates an object in our culture and thus misrepresents the IT, which is not an object. When we are aware, we are usually aware of something. It is well presented, at least in its early stages of spiritual development, in Thich Nhat Hanh's book *The Keys of Zen*. In my teaching I use several extracts, some directly from the manual he used in his novitiate as a young Buddhist monk. *The Little Manual* gives some very cogent teachings about what he termed "Awareness of being," which seems more akin to my understanding of awareness.

> I remember a short conversation between the Buddha and a philosopher of his time. The philosopher said, "I have heard you tell of Buddhism as a doctrine of enlightenment. What is the method? In other words, what do you do every day?" Shakyamuni replied, "We talk, wash ourselves, sit down . . ." The philosopher broke in: "What is there that is special in these actions? Everyone talks, eats, bathes, sits down." Shakyamuni said, "Sir, there is a difference. When we talk, we are aware of the fact that we talk, and so on. When others talk, eat, bathe, or sit down, they are not aware of what they do."

Perhaps this is the source of the famous reply to the charge that practitioners are involved in esoteric pursuits only, when the Zen Master said, "In reality, Zen *Roshis* are only selling water by the river."

The Little Manual says this of practicing Zen:

> In the monastery, the practitioner does everything; he carries water, he looks for firewood, prepares food, cultivates the garden etc. Although he learns to sit in the Zen position,

and to practise concentration and meditation in this position, he must strive to remain constantly aware of being
even when he carries water, cooks food, or cultivates the
garden. He knows that to carry water is not only a useful
action, it is also to practise Zen. If one does not know how
to practise Zen while carrying water, it is useless to live in a
monastery.

So carry-ing water is not something special, it is something
sacred. In another place, Thich Nhat Hanh says of *The Little
Manual*:

The practitioner does seemingly the same things as those
who do not practise the Way. If, for example, the student
shuts the door in a noisy way, he thus proves that he is not
aware of his being. Virtue does not consist in the fact of
closing the door gently, but in awareness of the fact that he
is in the process of closing the door. In this case, the master
simply summons his student and reminds him that he must
close the door and be mindful of it. He does this, not only
in order that the silence of the monastery can be respected,
but also to show the Way of Zen.

In recent years, more and more Western writers refer to
the psychological meaning of awareness where it is relegated
to the present moment. In his writing on the Enneagram, Riso
has some different thoughts. He says awareness is an important
term and has many different approaches to psychological and
spiritual growth. He thinks it is perhaps easier to be described
by what it is not: not thinking, not feeling, not intuition, not
moving, not instinct. Riso says it is usually taken up with our
inner talk, and that with more awareness, we are able to step
back from our imaginary conversation and critique it. He ends
by saying, "When we relax and allow awareness to expand, we
become less caught up in whatever has magnetized our
attention. If we have been fearful or anxious or lost in daydreams
and fantasies, we will gain objectivity and perspective about
what we are doing. We will suffer less."

Zen offers the same therapeutic effect, but as a fruit of sitting, and of silence. Those who want to develop the ability to practice awareness of being, the conduit for making connections, must go into silence. After putting the body in the best position for silence, we then do the same for the mind. The Oriental way of achieving this is not to activate the psyche. This process starts with breath-awareness, for beginners by counting the breaths. "Every effort at doing this paves the way for the spirit within to return to its original spontaneity," as one of the ancient Chinese masters phrased it. After a deep *kensho,* which temporarily obliterates the I, the I expands to IT.

On our cushion, we do the practice assigned by the teacher. Away from the cushion, we are aware of being. More simply but not completely, it can be said to mean that we are where we are, and we do what we are doing. For instance, if we are washing dishes, our body and mind are absorbed in harmony and open to connections while performing that task. I teach that awareness is part of openness. Let us not forget that we practice the opposite, which is separation, if we allow the mind to wander.

There is no problem when we are doing intellectual or artistically absorbing work. If we are solving geometrical problems, we just solve them. But when we put them aside and go out to sweep leaves, we so often still keep doing geometry in our heads, which is something that is not only permitted in Western culture but often is actually encouraged. There is something about Western culture that praises this. In Oriental spirituality it is frowned upon, because in this way we are separating mind and body.

Separation is the archenemy of all life. Indeed, the word "diabolical" is from the Greek *diabellein,* to separate or divide. So, separation is the work of the devil, and let us do away with it. In all our waking moments, let us try to be where we are, and not separated from the work or play in which we are engaged. When we complete one task, we drop it cleanly and completely, and proceed to the next encounter.

As Christians in prayer, we are not unused to silencing ourselves away from our work, whether physical or mental, as we relate to the transcendental God through mind and heart, memory and imagination. This is our tradition and it is as old as Christendom, and beyond as well. We are rational beings, and our relationships are nourishing for both mind and heart. It is our invaluable heritage, eloquently attested to in Western art, culture and religions. But we also have the heritage of contemplation (with little or no use of words) of the great doctor of Christian prayer, John of the Cross, and Meister Eckhart, and Tauler and many others.

Even in the novitiate, I had read John of the Cross's insistence that to really meditate, one had to suspend the use of our spiritual and physical senses, but I really didn't understand the implications. Meister Eckhart came into my life rather late. His enthronement of non-attachment and letting go are prescriptions I had been practicing and preaching for years. He turned out to be a popular referral. Eckhart identifies this spiritual happening of connections as the eternal birth which is always happening. To be available as recipient, one must go into training, which he says means that one must learn to act without attachment. We must let go. And the teaching of Eckhart's disciple Tauler was quoted frequently by Father Lassalle: "Diligent practice in the end demands one should sink down into the deepest ground. In those depths become that nothingness."

Zen is a state of consciousness beyond subject and object, and therefore not dual or relational. I used to feel the word "communion" was apt in describing Zen prayer, but now I feel perhaps "participating" is closer to what is happening. One's whole being is unimpededly infused with the divine power which is constant and everlasting. In a deep *kensho* experience, the "I" becomes absorbed in the IT. The joy of the raindrop is to enter the water.

When I entered the convent in 1953, it was almost impossible to find a teacher for guidance in contemplation. At best, one was told that mystical prayer is God's gift and one can only ask for it. I was fortunate enough to find the de Jaegher book, which started me on the silent path. But the Christian path was then awash with color and signs that kept me busy, happy and hopeful as I recorded them. For contemplative prayer, however, I had to come to the Orient to learn that there *are* teachers in the Way of silence, and that there is a practice which will lead to mystical experience.

The first step for a Christian doing Zen is to agree to leave behind the world of subject and object. No books are helpful in this kind of meditation, for when we seize one in the chapel or our place of prayer, we are just exchanging objects. We have, for the time being, to stop living in the head, since this is to live in the past or the future. The Orient tells us that now is the only reality, the past has gone and the future will never come. All we have is here and now.

The whole of Zen discipline is to make us come alive to the present. When we are sitting in *zazen*, breath-awareness is preliminary, and can sweep away thoughts. BE the breathing in and out, and eventually breathing (in meditation) will be BE-ING. Not to think but to BE is the secret of Zen. Relax and enjoy breathing, though be in awe. We have Scripture's word that it is the *Ruah,* the breath of God. I understand there is a Filipino saying, "When we die, God's breath is taken back." In the meantime, let us marvel at the mystery that we are!

As we advance in awareness and openness of be-ing, and gain some control over our active mind while we sit, gradually stillness and a certain equanimity take over. Very soon we feel better on the days we meditate, and more scattered if, for some reason or other, we cannot sit.

The therapeutic effects of mature sitting are well known. Our dissipated energies gradually become more unified, and we really start to gain some control over our superactive mind. Tensions are released, nerves become unfrayed, and physical health generally improves. Emotions are sensitized, and the will strengthened. We begin to experience a kind of inner balance, and gradually dryness, rigidity, hang-ups, prejudices and egotism melt and give way to compassion, serenity, egolessness and social concern. This is transformation indeed, although it does not happen the week after we start sitting. It is a lifelong endeavor.

There seems to be a general inherent expectation of transformation in prayer. It has been my experience over the last 40 years that more significant changes in the psyche occur in the practice of meditation than in prayers of petition. This is not to denigrate the same factor in relational prayer, which uses the psyche and can promote change there. We certainly feel better after a heart-to-heart talk with Jesus. Over the last 75 years, he has become a good and constant friend to me, and always available. Sometimes when I sit quietly I am drawn into the depths which is God, and then the "two" relationship comes to an end. The raindrop enters the ocean.

Personality changes are also effected by Zen. It may be a prayer of the desert, but perhaps that is where changes occur after all. We cannot expect to mature spiritually if we keep our prayer at the objective stage, and accompany it with words. Thoughts and feelings hold inordinate sway over us, and using the imagination is now very popular in the alternative disciplines and therapies. They are all much warmer and more colorful than the desert. But prayer will not normally produce transforming results as long as it is in the "doing and saying" stage.

It is the inner power of the Spirit in the dynamic unifying silence that changes us. That we can commune with God in silence and call it prayer is new for most Christians today. Although there is a growing distrust of verbiage, there is still some discomfort with total silence. In an unpublished manuscript, the late Fr. Lassalle said:

> Object meditation is becoming so unpopular that there is even some question as to the validity of starting beginners with it. In many Oriental countries, prayer is started at the super-object stage. This is particularly true of those countries that have had the least contact with the West. Occidentals are today aware of a strong new trend to the mysticism which is an experience of God. Zen Meditation is exactly the supra-object meditation which leads to an experience of faith and God. Any present exposé of the new person's spirituality which misses this point is drawing but a partial profile. People calling themselves Christians today must be prepared to expect an attraction to prayer in depth and not on the surface.

One of the ideograms chosen to represent the reality of Zen carries the message of "infinite," "simple," and connotes "offering," which give a more adequate explanation of Zen's "connecting" function. *Dhyana* (meditation) certainly sprang into new prominence following the enlightenment experience of Siddhartha Gautama, whose story is told in chapter 3.

In Zen orientation, when a person awakens to their inner Reality, the teacher will mention the word *Tathagata,* which Shakyamuni is said to have uttered after his awakening. Literally it means "just as comes, just as goes" and connotes the state of perfection. Everything just as it comes and goes is pure and undefiled. Whatever the phenomenal limitation, the Essential is without blemish.

It is with considerable dissatisfaction that I use the word "perfect" because it is usually judgmental and dichotomizing, in the sense that it presupposes its opposite, "imperfect." Zen has to do with the world of non-duality, which transcends both perfect and imperfect. Perhaps for Christians this is not abstruse, because we refer to God as good and perfect, with no possible connotation of the opposite. In any case, the world of the empty-Infinite vivifies all of creation. There are several exclamations frequently lauding this reality heard in Zen halls: "The radiance permeates the whole universe."

In 1976, I was posted to the Philippines, because our community had ended its mission work in Japan. I made the trip by boat, and many friends came to Kobe to wish me well. The custom of throwing spools of colored ribbon to people as they leave was new to me. Thus I found myself holding 15 or 20 strands, with the other end each held by one of those friends, and I suddenly realized how much all these people had contributed not only to my being able to live in the difficult Zen program, but also to mature as a human being in reflective love and justice. Then the ribbons began to break, one by one, as the boat pulled out into the Pacific Ocean. I thought I heard a little snap in my heart as each one broke.

RELUCTANCE

Out through the fields and the woods
And over the walls I have wended;
I have climbed the hills of view
And looked at the world and descended;
I have come by the highway home,
And lo, it is ended.
The leaves are all dead on the ground,
Save those that the oak is keeping
To ravel them one by one
And let them go scraping and creeping
Out over the crusted snow,
When others are sleeping.
And the dead leaves lie huddled and still,
No longer blown hither and thither;
The last lone aster is gone;
The flowers of the witch-hazel wither;
The heart is still aching to seek,
But the feet question "Whither?"
Ah, when to the heart of man
Was it ever less than a treason,
To go with the drift of things,
To yield with a grace to reason,
And bow and accept the end
Of a love or a season?

Robert Frost

I lived in Manila for a year, where I went to language school, and at the invitation of the country's outstanding theologian, Fr. Catalino Arevalo S.J., I started teaching Zen. By November, we had about 30 sitters and a chapel in which to sit, so we organized a formal installation of the Manila Zen Center on November 21, 1976. Father Arevalo spoke at the mass, and his opening sentences were: "Today is the Feast of Christ the King. Every particle of creation is filled with the beauty of Christ, the love of Christ, the truth of Christ, and the goodness of Christ." I couldn't help but think most Buddhists would feel at home with that statement.

Teilhard de Chardin says the same thing in his Hymn of the Universe: "Maker of the Universe, teach me to adore it by seeing you hidden within. Say once again to me, Lord, those great and liberating words, that are at once revealing light and effective poem – *Hoc est corpus meum* – this is my body."

In Buddhist temples, one frequently sees a statue of Shakyamuni emerging from his experience and reaching down as though to touch the earth. This signifies his desire to return to the phenomenal world where he could help people come to terms with their suffering. As the result of the experience, he was compelled to go out to people and help them shed the shackles keeping them bound, which he found to be the cause of suffering. Shakyamuni subsequently spent the rest of his life in this kind of service to people.

And that is what Zen is all about. It is to experience *Tathagata* of the universe and then to respond appropriately to our world and its violence, injustice, poverty and pollution. Shakyamuni did not just sit. His experience seemed to propel him into action for others. Yamada Roshi used to say if you cannot sympathize with another, there is no *satori*. Experience realizes itself in involvement. Having found peace, we return peace in service.

At the turn of the decade, I heard a Jesuit specialist analyzing the community's efforts to be agents of social change during the last decade. He admitted that on the whole, the program had failed. An analysis pointed to the fact that change requires process, and personal transformation has to happen before a person can effect change for the better. Social justice and sustainable development cannot happen only on the intellectual level or by an act of the will. They must evolve from a deeper space. Zen has been saying that for centuries.

So when we start to meditate, we are determined to reach that space. We leave all our learning and accomplishments, as well as troubles and worries, at the gate. We put ourselves humbly but confidently and with great personal determination in the hands of a qualified teacher. Gradually, we experience the unifying process of Zen practice, and the benefits that accrue from it.

The discipline is not easy. When I started at Enkoji Temple, in the early 1960s, during retreat after only three hours of sleep, we rose at 3:00 a.m. and started chanting five minutes later. The Buddhist nuns sleep in their underclothes, and have only to put on their outer robe when they rise. For them, five minutes is quite sufficient for dressing, a quick face wash, and toilet privileges before morning chants. Being in the long habit at the time, I needed to use those precious five minutes getting into the various layers. I didn't get my face washed for three days, and spent many an uncomfortable hour until an appropriate break time to use the loo. (One uses that place of convenience rather often when sitting in the lotus position.) There were six toilets just outside the *zendo* at Enkoji. After each use, we washed our hands out of doors, using a bamboo ladle and water from a picturesque well carved in a rock. I found in the winter, after breaking the ice which had formed on the top, one tended to lose one's appreciation of the culture.

There was no heat available anywhere outside the kitchen and one guest room. Rinzai Zen is tough.

Before I left Japan, my monk friend Horisawa San invited me to accompany him and his group of Buddhists on a pilgrimage to the holy places in India. It proved to be a great privilege which deepened my Zen experience and also added enormously to my life adventures. I don't think anyone could ever be prepared for one's first trip to India. We landed in Calcutta in the dark, and outstretched palms were visible, as were shining white teeth and eyes when we looked up. Beggars, beggars, everywhere. I was overwhelmed. Our guide counseled us not to give indiscriminately. Eventually, as we saw some of the apparent disabled discard their crutches at the end of the day before they went home, we decided to make a daily donation to a group that supported the beggars.

I felt happily at home in the many Christian churches we found. Also, the Hindu temples had some explanations written in English, which I certainly appreciated. My problem was trying to adjust to Indian art in the shrines, which I found hideous in color and riotous in detail. I was so used to the Kamakura *Daibutsu* (the large statue of the Buddha), which is strong in its poverty of un-essentials, and full of mysterious peace.

We missed Buddha's birthplace, Lumbini (Nepal), because its airport was not yet open. But we went to Bodhigaya, Sarnath, Deer Park and the other famous places in this other Holy Land, India.

But before any of these, we went first to Nagpur, in the center of the country, where we stayed for almost a week. It was important for Horisawa San because his friend had come from Japan to do a severe training there. His friend rarely joined us, as he was recuperating from very bad burns he had inflicted upon himself on the back of each hand in a penitential rite.

They seemed to be festering in the Indian heat. Horisawa San had endured that penance some years before, and still wears an ugly scar on his upper right arm.

Horisawa San also used that week to give his only religious exhortation during the tour. It was of two hours duration, and was given in a kind of stadium that many centuries before had been a place of debate in early Buddhism. At that time, there was a solemn debate by adherents to the two evolving schools of thought, one cherishing the letter of the law while the opponent was on fire to travel and take Shakyamuni's words to other countries. Thus the shades of Hinayana and Mahayana, the Small Vehicle and the Large Vehicle. Meanwhile, the new religion remained in the hands of the upper classes in India, and by the seventh century, had died out in the country of its birth.

At the time of our visit there was almost no available water in Nagpur. None in the toilets, none in the sinks, and of course none of the showers or baths were operating. We took our face cloths into meals and moistened them from the drinking water, which of course we didn't dare drink. I recall two events resulting from that situation. First, I went hunting for a hairdresser for a hair wash. The man did the complete job with water that filled one 26-ounce bottle of Gordon's gin. On my return to the hotel, I passed an archway on which was written "St. Margaret's Convent." I went through the grounds and rang the convent bell. The sisters were delightful, congratulating me for being out of the habit, and urging me to stay and teach music at their school in Simla (the Indian equivalent to Banff, Alberta). I was all fired up with the possibility of bringing Zen back to India. I requested this when I eventually returned to Toronto, but it didn't work out.

That evening in Nagpur, after supper, Horisawa San, who himself had lived in this area for five years in ascetic training, asked if I would accompany him to bathe in an outdoor spring that he remembered in the district. Used to his daily *ofuro* (bath), he sought a good soak to wash away the remnants of the heat and subsequent perspiration. There were many baths in the local area which came from underwater springs that kept bubbling up to the surface of the earth, and they are often used by local shepherds who come each evening for a pleasant social hour.

I gave much thought to what to wear. I had read, but had yet to witness, that women bathed in the Ganges, and the exposure of any bare skin was forbidden. I had in my suitcase all-encompassing thermal-wear, because our trip included Katmandu and a possible flight to Everest. I also had a voluminous kaftan. The question was, which would I wear in the water? I settled on the underwear, threw the kaftan over top, stuffed in a long slip in case there was some kind of an emergency, and feeling like a mannequin in an itinerant tent, I set off with the bald-headed monk.

The topography reminded me of Saskatchewan, open fields with very little undulation. The stars were plentiful in the wide night sky, and the partial moon gave us all the light we required. Not a house or animal or human being was in sight. In due time, we arrived at the edge of a large, sunken pond, which was half filled with steaming water. There were some flaming torches in the ground along the rim of the pool. At our feet was a broad set of steps and on our right a receptacle of water. Most importantly, there were 25 or 30 pairs of eyes watching us. At first I was so stunned I couldn't move. They were all men and all seemed naked. I hadn't counted on those factors. But without any ado, Horisawa San stripped, threw some of the water over his body, and walked down the steps to the greetings of the men, who appeared to recall who he was.

Then they all looked at me. I was still frozen on the top step. Finally, with a now-or-never abandon, I shed the kaftan and donned the long slip because I was psychologically unable to parade down the avenue wearing only a pair of long johns. I threw some water up in the air, and descended into the muddy pool; all the while the men observed wide-eyed and silent.

Once the intensity of the curiosity lessened, Horisawa San told them I was from Canada. The shepherds immediately wanted to hear my country's song. So in that wide-open arena, under the starry Indian sky, all the while thinking that nobody would ever believe the story of this adventure (indeed, hardly believing it myself), I belted out *O Canada* to the Indian shepherds and Japanese monk. They loved the rhythm and swayed in time. They nodded approval. Then they asked Horisawa San to sing his country's song. Being tone deaf he asked me to sing along, and together we sang the sad, mournful tune *"Kimi ga Yo."* This was followed by a respectful silence. And then we were treated to a medley of local songs with everyone applauding each rendition. Canada seemed a little closer that night.

What a rich life. And a rich prayer life in parallel. But do we measure by the highs or lows? There is a wonderful *koan* which asks, "Which is higher, Mount Fuji or Mount Everest?" And when the interviewee starts to give that exasperated look which says "anyone would know *that*," the Zen teacher interrupts, "Only a fool would say Mount Everest!"

We plug away with our sitting, with our *dokusan* (interview) responses, and some day when, as Yamada Roshi used to say, all things are ready (perhaps at a time least expected), we break through the barrier and "shake the earth and astonish the heavens." We find that heaven is not beyond the clouds at all, and God is closer to me than I am to myself. Or in the words of Zen Master Hakuin: "This very place is the Lotus Land, this very body the Buddha." The hidden pearl of great price will be discovered through personal experience in contemplation. Anyone faithful to daily practice will one day reap its joyful dividends.

Chapter Six

From Intellect to Breath

Music was my profession for decades. Over those years it became increasingly more transcendent. I was first made aware of this possibility of transcendence one day at the Juilliard School of Music in New York. Waiting outside the teacher's studio for my weekly lesson, I was suddenly accosted by a young man who came along the corridor. To my surprise he stopped in front of me, put his two hands on my shoulders and shook them, demanding, "There is a God, isn't there!" I smiled and replied that if he just looked out of the window he would find every indication that that is so. He released his grip and spread his arms out wide, saying, "If there isn't, then none of this would make sense, would it!" Not a question but a statement. He was not carrying an instrument, so perhaps he was a composition major. Lots of frustrations and disappointments in that field. But he seemed to nudge that transcendent door for me.

Through my teenage years, I was not aware that music and God were so cohesive. But the connection became an underpinning. I cannot remember when I started presuming I would have music as my profession. Going back a few years, when I was about 10, it was decided I should begin lessons at Mount Allison Conservatory with my mother's friend and former associate, Cladie Smith. Every Saturday I boarded the local bus for the hour trip. I cannot recall any high or low points, except when people asked if I found studying at Mount Allison interesting, I remarked that the drugstore in which I waited for the return bus trip was owned by two men whose names were Leak and Gas! True.

But during the gap year between high school and university there were significant changes. My whole world expanded because of the fine books and teaching and other events which were part of my life then. God became an intellectual pursuit, which I found rather attractive. I started to wonder if perhaps philosophy might be possible for my university studies. As far as music was concerned, I knew I would never be able to play the violin like David Oistrach, whose warm tones I found especially moving. Music certainly comes from the heart and gives expression to our whole being, but I found over time that my attitude toward music became ambivalent, as I experienced less opportunity for sport and substituted voracious reading during those precious hours instead. In my philosophical pursuit, I would follow head rather than heart, although I realized, and cherished the fact, that the latter gives impetus to melody and harmony. When I talked this over with my surprised parents, they asked me what I thought philosophy was. I had to answer truthfully that I really didn't know. The final decision was that I would get my Licentiate of Music in two years at Mount Allison and then make the decision on my own.

In 1942, there were not many incentives and perks for young musicians. Mount Allison did well, though, and provided us with many opportunities to perform locally. The

Conservatory sponsored concerts all over the Maritimes, in which the students performed, sometimes in proper auditoriums, other times in much more modest halls. The programs of music we presented were of the same compositions as the great artists who appeared at the university's main auditorium, Fawcett Hall. This was always appreciated by the audiences.

Interesting circumstances prevailed as well. For one concert, Mary Connelly, a piano major student, and I gave a recital in Little Shimogue, New Brunswick. Following our rehearsal that afternoon in the Oulton Corner Church Hall, I decided to go for a long walk alone through the fields, which were still in stubble. Gradually, I became aware of being followed, and when I turned around to look, there were 24 turkeys in line, all keeping step with me!

Another time, I was chosen to be co-recitalist with Mount Allison's Assistant English Professor and singer, Albert Trueman, known to his friends as Bud. A man who was often referred to as a Mandarin, Bud was educated at Oxford. After his stint at Mount Allison, he became President of the University of Manitoba, President of the University of New Brunswick, Chairman of the National Film Board, and Director of the Canada Council. He held innumerable chancellorships and trusteeships, and was made a Companion in the Order of Canada in June 1974. Quite a man!

I'll recount one adventure with him. Along with his attractive personality (and aren't most singers actually actors?) he had a splendid baritone voice and was a wonderful storyteller. As we were being driven to the recital hall in Saint John, New Brunswick, we chatted in the car, and he asked about the course I was taking in creative writing. After declaiming about subject matter, he related his experience as a freshman English major. There was an assignment to write a short story. Bud situated his tale on the high seas in the south Pacific, in which adventures abounded. He did not receive commendation for the effort and the accompanying note was cryptic. "Write about something you know." So his next assignment was entitled *Blue Roses*. Bud was color blind! His hearty laugh filled the car that evening, and I remember giving him one long hard look, hoping to discover the source of his love of life. There wasn't a smell of philosophy about him!

I followed his career with great interest, and was able to renew our acquaintance several years later when, as head of the Canada Council for the Arts, he came to St. Catharines, Ontario, and opened a cultural center there.

PRAYER OF THE COCK

Do not forget, Lord,
it is I who make the sun rise.
I am your servant
but, with the dignity of my calling,
I need some glitter and ostentation.
Noblesse oblige . . .
All the same,
I am your servant
Only . . . do not forget, Lord,
I make the sun rise.

(From *Prayers from the Ark*, poems by Carmen Bernos de Gastold & Rumer Godden)

The books I devoured in that wonderful gap year were mainly from Europe, very Catholic and contemporary. They were the three Ms of France – Jacques Maritain, François Mauriac, André Maurois – and the three Bs of England – Hillaire Belloc's *Path to Rome*, Maurice Baring's *In my End is my Beginning*, and Hugh Benson's very popular *Come Rack!*

Come Rope! These authors and their works brought me into human depths and ultimately into myself. I had not read many books that concentrated solely on one individual, bringing the reader right into the mind and heart of that person. Their books warmed the heart of philosophy. The characters became bigger than life because they inevitably triumphed in the end. They were people who struggled, suffered, lived and loved passionately, and who somehow, despite despair, never fully abandoned their center of the Sacred. I do wonder why I read so little of Chesterton, because he was to find me in later life. I now use some of his ideas and phrases when I give *teisho* (Zen public talks). But at that time, I was too captivated with the flow of life and the glow of love to be open to his more cerebral genius. Belloc was a particular favorite. His biographies were breathtaking. He wrote of people the way Renoir paints them and sets them aglow. They seemed to view human beings as God must surely see them, I thought. And not just people. One image I will never forget is Belloc's allotting roles to flowers: "and sweet peas will sing the hymns in church."

For that year, at home we kept a card table set up in our house. Mother, Olwin and I were ardent bridge players, and when the doorbell rang, we had two thoughts in mind: a cup of tea and a rubber of bridge. As I reflect on my early years, I marvel at and am grateful for the very foundations of family and home life which we enjoyed. Even as children, we had amazing freedom, especially outside the house. I find it difficult to grasp a sense of the necessity present-day parents feel in always having to have their children within eyesight. During holidays, we would run out of the house after breakfast, and not come home until the noon meal. We also had the run of the town all afternoon. I recall our evening playtime was usually in our own backyard, but otherwise the whole area was our playground.

Meals were quite another thing. Food was never slapped together and thrown on the table. We always had a cook, but Mother inspected everything that was put on the table. Noon was the main meal, and our parents and grandfather ate alone in peace. We children were allowed to be noisy when we ate an hour earlier. Brother Bill was a constant tease. He kept inventing gruesome tales about what was in the food we were eating. Snakes were his common reference. It must have got through to Ethel because even in adulthood, when she is troubled by nightmares, they invariably concern snakes.

The war years brought the accompanying restrictions, but still Mother provided me with the opportunity to plan and execute a dinner party for 12. Her china was Limoges and of a restrained but truly lovely design. The size of napkin and the amount of silver to be displayed and used (our Old English pattern) were important issues. The menu was discussed endlessly, it seemed: how to save ration coupons so a decent dessert could be served, what wines would be appropriate, and so on. All was of my own choosing, under her watchful eye, but within the customs of Moncton in that era.

I recount these things because I see now they were the raw material of the spiritual I was learning in the process of appreciating the beautiful and the good. It involves being exposed to variety. In food, for instance, it meant becoming informed of quality and nutrition and taste, making decisions about circumstances of time and place and people, and generally learning the appropriateness of the different items on the menu. In food, too, "every particle of creation is filled with God." It was some years before I was to become a fan of the author Robertson Davies, but I grew to admire his characters. They so often possessed total integrity. I seemed to have imbibed his logic: if we continuously use words like "shit," then that is the kind of person we will become.

Following that wonderful year, Juilliard beckoned. And from that moment, until I entered the convent almost 10 years later, I was inspired and encouraged by three individuals, two of whom were also seeking to find their life vocation in the light of that young music student at Juilliard. If there is no God, then it all doesn't make sense. My mother was very friendly with a group of her MacNeil cousins, all of whom lived in the States. Alma MacNeil had married a brilliant Italian doctor, and I was invited to live with them in Teaneck, New Jersey, while studying at Juilliard. I formed a special friendship with their younger son, Bill. He was seven years my junior and the younger brother I had always wanted. I delighted in watching him spend hours sprucing up before a mirror, adjusting his loud tie with the large bow, and plastering his hair down close to the scalp. I was occasionally invited into his circle of friends, who called me Miss Canada and took me for my first visit to a pizza parlor. The pies were the size of the table, almost a meter in diameter!

Despite our age difference, we had much in common. Bill, who has since become a distinguished and internationally known cardiologist, also likes music, a fact I have reflected on during my last visit to his home in Marlboro, Massachusetts. We sat together for hours watching an impressive symphony orchestra playing some Beethoven and the Tchaikovsky violin concerto with Megumi San as soloist. It was one of those moments of perfect contentment with a friend.

THE PRAYER OF THE GOAT

Lord,
Let me live as I will!
I need a little wild freedom,
A little giddiness of heart,
The strange taste of unknown flowers.
For whom else are your mountains?
Your snow wind? These springs?
The sheep do not understand.
They graze and graze,
All of them, and always in the same direction,
And then eternally
Chew the cud of their insipid routine.
But I . . . I love to bound to the heart of all
Your marvels,
Leap your chasms,
And in my mouth stuffed with intoxicating grasses
Quiver with an adventurer's delight
On the summit of the world.

(From *Prayers from the Ark*, poems by Carmen Bernos de Gastold & Rumer Godden)

By 1943, I was having thought-provoking experiences at Juilliard. It was very expensive studying there, and one day, a notice went up that a famous All Girl Orchestra was looking for violinists. A couple of days later, a small group of fiddlers met in one of the rooms. Two had gone downtown to audition and had been told immediately they would be expected to sleep with the conductor if they passed the audition. One girl turned around and walked out. The other told us she really needed the money and signed on.

There was also the expected rivalry. The first day one young fiddler invited a group of us into his practice room to demonstrate the speed and clarity of his up-bow staccato. He was challenged by someone else, and so it continued. Not feeling at all competitive, I left the room and bumped into a rather rotund Italian tenor, who started to weep on my shoulder that he had not passed his entrance exam. He apparently had been in the army, and after honorable discharge was determined to study voice at Juilliard. He was depressed enough for suicide that day.

Juilliard and New York were a great experience. Although the school was not as yet in its new location at Lincoln Center, I still loved the ambience of 121st Street, between Broadway and Riverside Drive. It was a stone's throw from the little church where Thomas Merton had been instructed and baptized. The carillons in the famous Riverside Drive Church must have chimed themselves into my very soul. Years later when giving *teisho* (Zen talk) in the Philippines, I called on them to ease the distance between the Manila Zendo and the Temple bell in Japan. (Now there's a *koan*, beyond intellectual understanding!) I also enjoyed the invigorating company of several articulate musicians when, on the suggestion of my teacher Louise Behrend, I enrolled in the Music Criticism class at Columbia University, just down the street. Ashley Pettis was the instructor. He eventually became a convert and priest, which surprised us all. During his absence, Virgil Thompson took over the class, and was appropriately regarded by us as the height of sophistication. His opera *The Mother of Us All* had just been performed and proved to be genuinely American.

There was lots of listening enjoyment as well. Fritz Kreisler's last concert at Carnegie Hall. Judy Garland's last appearance on stage in New York. My own teacher at a summer concert in Central Park. Scintillating jazz on the lawn of one of the libraries at Columbia University. And several concerts on the stages in Juilliard itself.

Returning to the Castelli home in Teaneck each night and talking with Bill or his mother, I was able to articulate and integrate my experiences of the day into perspective. Despite our age difference, Bill and I were both facing life decisions. Although it didn't become evident for a few years, we both felt we wanted a grounding in philosophy as part of our future life endeavors. In the end, I went on to Calgary and into the hands of a budding philosopher. Bill went on to Yale, the alma mater of his father, to study pre-med, but just as importantly Bill had in mind that he wanted to study with John Courtney Murray S.J. in the philosophy and religion classes there. He tells me they saved his vocation! This story is part of Bill's autobiography, which he wrote with Glen Griffin.

Once, Bill invited me to the Yale campus for a football game. The Yale Squad was playing Columbia, where I had studied, and he had bought a Columbia banner for me to wave. As champion of the Ivy League he took me to the stadium, dressed in a reserved tweed and clapping judiciously whenever Yale gained a few yards. He was a cool figure alongside my ostentatious cheers for Columbia, which were accompanied by enthusiastic banner waving.

Eventually Bill took his medical studies at Louvain in Belgium so that he might deepen his grasp of scholastic philosophy. He spent holiday-time travelling to rural areas with a group of like-minded youths, especially during religious festivals, to bring ordinary people the stimulation of music and prayer and fireside discussions about the meaning of life. Eventually he returned to the States an enormously enriched human being, chose to be a cardiologist, and soon became head of the largest heart research center in the world, the Framingham Institute near Boston, a position he held for 30 years. We have since met in places as far removed as Manila and Oxford as he takes his understanding of healthy living on world tours.

After New York, I went on to Calgary, in the foothills of the Rocky Mountains in Alberta. In time I grew to love them but at a distance. It is almost overpowering to live in their midst and a tendency to vertigo deterred me from scaling those heights. I have often wondered about my propensity to go deeply into things. It is always a downward thrust. It comes from the sea, perhaps. I never refer to the experiences in Zen as the heights of prayer. It is always the depths to which I feel called.

I played in the Calgary Symphony Orchestra. Clayton Hare, my former teacher at the Mount Allison Conservatory, was the conductor at the time. It was there that I had my one experience of playing under Sir Ernest MacMillan, a legendary figure in Canadian music history. The newly formed Edmonton Symphony Orchestra sent word they needed certain key players, one of which was a viola player, and I accepted the invitation to commute. I was employed by the Mount Royal College Conservatory as a violin teacher, and enjoyed that work very much.

At one point, I was asked to be concert master of a small orchestra accompanying a church group performing Gilbert and Sullivan's *Pirates of Penzance*. I was to be picked up, and the chauffeur turned out to be a very personable young man who had just returned from Notre Dame University with a philosophy degree. Next morning, the local newspaper contained the news that this man had been elected to the College edition of *Who's Who* for his intellectual and athletic brilliancy (he had been a member of Canada's Olympic track team). His name was Ernie McCullough, and he proved to be the philosopher I had been seeking.

We not only shared first desk in that orchestra, but also the ride to and from the numerous rehearsals, and many other points of common interest. I found Ernie's companionship a continuation of the kinds of times I had spent with my cousin Bill. We were both desperately involved in trying to decide our life's journey. Ernie's erudition, his humor, his easygoing manners, his patience with my innumerable preponderances were just what I needed. He, too, came from a musical family, and we had many musical soirees. We also played golf together, and I travelled with his family to their summer home in Eugene, Oregon.

One of my visits to their lovely Calgary home was the occasion of a dinner party for the Calgary Stampeders football team. While the drinks were being served, Ernie invited me to his room to see a pile of philosophical books that had just arrived. I remember turning to him and, in a manner which came out rather abruptly, asking him to relate in a sentence or two the main thesis of the most prominent philosophers beginning with Plato. He should have thrown the books at me. Instead he did precisely as I asked, and when he reached contemporary philosophers, I had had enough. I finally knew in my heart of hearts that philosophy was not what I was seeking. Despite its erudition over the ages, it had none of the answers I was searching for. It all seemed to be either propositions, questions or opinions. I longed for some kind of certitude. It was also at that point that Ernie made the suggestion that was to set me on my way: "Perhaps you are seeking the real thing."

One Christmas Eve, I approached the McCullough home on a hillock in Mount Royal. It was snowing slightly. Standing in the driveway under the portico, I heard heavenly music from within. I could distinguish at one point an organ and piano playing carols together, and when I entered the house, I found Mr. McCullough had just been given an organ by the family, and his youngest daughter Barbara was duetting with him on the grand piano. How beautiful could life get?

PRAYER OF THE DOVE

The Ark waits
Lord,
The Ark waits on Your will
And the sign of Your peace.
I am the dove
simple
as the sweetness that comes from You.
The Ark waits
Lord
It has endured.
Let me carry it
A sprig of hope and joy,
And put, at the heart of its forsakenness,
This, in which Your love clothes me,
Grace immaculate.
Amen.

(From *Prayers from the Ark*, poems by Carmen Bernos de
Gastold & Rumer Godden)

In 1998, 47 years after leaving Calgary, I returned. After a
teaching career at the University of Saskatchewan, Ernie retired
to Calgary. He asked me to speak at the new university where
he was doing some lecturing. It was amazing to find not only
him but also Mr. Hare, my former teacher and symphony
conductor, and my accompanist Marie Meyers Barber there
to greet me. The introduction was given by Ernie, who made
the point that I had come full circle. It happily seemed so.

Music has played a great part in my life and it has been
interesting for me to note that so many people who had a
profound influence on me generally loved music. Yamada Roshi
was one; as for most Japanese music lovers of his day, Beethoven
was his great favorite. I discovered there is such a thing as a

national temperament. I personally felt I played Brahms well, especially in public. There is a broad romantic sweep to his compositions, and when playing for others, I always seemed to have a surplus of energy and was grateful to have it absorbed in performing one of the Brahms Sonatas. Larry MacGarrell, my accompanist in Japan, used to say, though, that he thought I played French music best.

It is difficult to describe music with words, but my most sublime moment in my profession happened when I was at Juilliard. We instrumentalists were assigned to an orchestra and a chamber music group for rehearsals. At that time, Juilliard had its first resident quartet, with Arthur Winograd as cellist. He was the assigned teacher to the piano quartet in which I was first violinist. We were quite an international group. Anna the pianist was from Hong Kong, Ginny the violist was from the American West, Floyd the cellist was from Florida. And I was a Canadian.

We were working on one of the Brahms piano quartets, Opus 25, in G Minor. The slow movement is especially beautiful. The melody joins heaven and the human soul in the most stirring and satisfying plea, with cello as solo. It begins with a descending passage, of utmost beauty and sensitivity. This opening statement is fairly long, with the cello soaring above the other instruments in a continuous flow . . . a delicious Brahmsian melody. Over and over again, the heart reaches out for its other self with deep sonorous tones, and the piano and viola and violin in a moving accompaniment. Brahms at his most eloquent! When the cello has finished its singing, the violin takes over. The movement is an elegant interplay of all the instruments weaving in and out and through, the tone color of each instrument having its moment to shine.

Our student cellist was not quite up to the potential of the music. Winograd listened through it once, and then showed the cellist a few points. However, the student was unable to execute the subtleties, so in a kind of artistic exuberance that could not be silenced, Winograd took his own instrument and asked the rest of us to play with him. Accompanying his artistry and exquisite tone, we each played our heart out. All the elements that go into a perfect performance seemed to appear, and I thought my heart would burst from sheer beauty and joy. I lost myself in it completely. The way to find the self is to lose the self, as I was to discover later in Zen. Perhaps there is a parallel in Luke 17:33: "Anyone who tries to preserve his life will lose it; and anyone who loses it will keep it safe."

Looking back, it is not surprising that Yamada Roshi always said he was happy when disciples came to him from the arts. They seemed already out of the head and digging into transcendence. One of his explanations of the Zen process was that the famous *Mu koan* most often given to beginners in their sitting is like a small electric drill that the meditator holds up to the sheet of thick black glass that seemingly separates us from the transcendence. Eventually there is a breakthrough.

Does Zen practice incline a practitioner to music of a certain kind or era? I don't think so. Zen doesn't try to make us into some special kind of person. Zen makes us free. Zen would have us not practice in order to build up a great program either of design or action. Yamada Roshi used to remind the *aikido* students who came to sit at our *dojo* that Zen would help them in their practice, that their art is a disciple of Zen and not the other way around. Even in argument or teaching, Zen tells us to be stripped of all concepts. In his teaching of the Hensho Goi No. 3 from the last book of *koan* studies, Yamada Roshi translates the meaning of Tozan's verse as, "If concepts have been extinguished completely, then you may say anything as freely as you will . . . even for example, if it is so subtle as to be beyond expression, beyond saying, beyond putting into words . . . speak out! And if concepts have been extinguished, your words will surpass the eloquence of the most eloquent of worldly men." Luke (21:14) tells us that Christ had somewhat the same concern: "Don't be concerned about what you are going to say, for I will give you the right words and such logic that none of your opponents will be able to reply."

Can music bring about a *kensho*, that experience which catapults us into the spiritual world? I suppose it could be the catalyst. It never was for me. But it certainly can unstick us from our usual sense perceptions. I can think of one great moment in Osaka, Japan, which illustrates that point. I went to hear the Philadelphia Orchestra with Eugene Ormandy conducting. The only seat I could get was the third from the front, which made me seem to be among the first violin section. At times I was confused as to whether or not I was playing with the orchestra. I had to sit on my hands for a while, to center myself in the audience. The Philadelphia Orchestra has often been called the virtuoso orchestra, and it certainly was that night. Its magic worked on me.

One person who had lived through the 1960s, those years of great change in North America, was the young Jesuit pianist Larry MacGarrell, who was another mainstay of mine during those years of searching. He, too, had been missioned to Japan and studied at the Jesuit Language School in Kamakura the same year I moved there to be close to Yamada Roshi. For three years, Larry and I practiced together every Thursday morning. We often gave command performances for the *Roshi* and his disciples; it was during one of these that the statement was made that my playing was no longer "only from muscle and ego."

In our Kamakura practice room, Larry and I chatted animatedly during our rest periods, and I learned about the many changes in our North American culture during the '60s and early '70s. In some ways, during my novitiate, juniorate and early years in Japan, when I did not have access to newspapers, radio or television, I often felt I was closeted, a veritable Rip Van Winkle for 20 years. My first tour of duty in Japan had lasted 6 years, a period that began in a long habit and ended in a simple dress.

Listening to Larry at first, I thought he was from another planet. But gradually I came to understand the seminal differences the '60s brought about. In some instances, I still feel conservative and old-fashioned. But the freer I become from my sitting, the less it matters. Larry joined the *Zendo*, came to experience and started *koan* study, so we had an enormous common ground. He was also better trained than I in theology and biblical studies, not to mention the Japanese language at which he soon excelled. He was generous with his gifts. The ease with which I slipped into teaching Zen in the predominantly Roman Catholic country of the Philippines was due in large part to the many hours he helped me think inconsistencies through to harmony in relating theory and practice in contemplation. I made several retreats with him, and had the freedom to meditate with a biblical phrase. Then, after running out of inferences, I could slip into Zen silence with the understanding approval of the retreat master!

PRAYER OF THE CRICKET

O God
I am little and very black,
But I thank you
For having shed
Your warm sun
And the quivering of your golden corn
On my humble life.
Then take – but be forbearing, Lord –
This little impulse of my love:
This note of music
You have set thrilling in my heart.

(From *Prayers from the Ark*, poems by Carmen Bernos de Gastold & Rumer Godden)

Christianity changed somewhat during the revolution of the '60s. But changes had been taking place for centuries. Although gradually being released from its bonds, the Judeo-Christian religion was for centuries frozen in Greek thought patterns, seeing people as an inferior body encompassing a superior soul. Now we are witnessing a revival of the ancient biblical and Hebraic philosophy. We are body, soul and spirit. Which puts us in sync with the Orient, too. We are coming to life again in our triune reality. We just might provide a reason for the phenomenon of the great numbers of Christians who are today turning to Oriental prayer methods and feeling they have come home.

In the beginning there was life, a breathing life. In biblical literature, a person is seen as a unity, which is viewed from three different aspects: in Hebrew they are *bashar* (flesh), related to earth; *nephesh* (soul), oriented to fellow beings; and *ruah* (breath of God), radically focused in God. "Then the LORD God formed man from the dust of the ground, and breathed into his nostrils a breath of life; and the man became a living being"(Genesis 2:7).

According to the Benedictine author Dom Wulstan, "a person is seen in the Bible as created for union, by a likeness to God that seeks union with like, with the breath of God within him acting as a link between them." This breathing-God was not unknown to John of the Cross (1542–81). Stanza 39 of his "Spiritual Canticle" speaks of this aspect of God in beautiful medieval phraseology:

> The breathing of the air is properly of the Holy Spirit, for which the soul here prays so that she may love God perfectly. She calls it the breathing of the air because it is a most delicate touch and feeling of love which habitually in this state is caused in the soul by the communion of the Holy Spirit. Breathing with His Divine Breath, He raises the soul most sublimely, and informs her that she may breathe in God the same breath of love that the Father breathes in the Son, and the Son in the Father, which is the same Holy Spirit that they breathe into her in the said transformation. And this is for the soul so high a glory, and so profound a delight, that it cannot be described by mortal tongue, nor can human understanding as such, attain to any conception of it.

A contemporary of mine in Japan, Thomas Woodward, expresses it this way:

> I think Eastern religions are onto something when they link prayer to the simple act of breathing, filling our lungs with the *ruah*, the Spirit of God, breathing the cosmic rhythm. The *pneuma*, the *ruah* of God, breathing right into our bodies, filling our lungs, making us live-spirited. How important it is to remember that an incredible power is surging up from the heart of the universe sweeping through the world like the wind, the Spirit of God. To be in touch with that power is always to have enough courage to deal creatively with the world around us.

And so in my Zen practice, although it took years, I moved from the intellect to the breath. If there is a shred of truth in all this teaching, how did we Christians ever get so sidetracked as to put our prayerful encounters with the Infinite so predominantly in the intellect? On the one hand, it is amazing that there is so little in classic and modern Christian literature about this other aspect of spirituality. Short phrases in the writings of the early Fathers lead us to believe that they practiced a similar kind of prayer.

On the other hand, it is quite evident that the complementary gift of Christianity to this evolving and universal spirituality is our relationship to the transcendental God. This is a real relationship, one that implies "the other." In our communication we address each other and we emote toward this "other" that is objective and to whom we feel we can relate. We are after all, relational beings. It is in realization of this that I point out the difference between Western and Oriental meditation. Christian meditation is in essence relational.

However, if seekers want a type of meditation that is both therapeutic and leading toward an experience, they must go to silence. In his writings and teaching, Anthony de Mello frequently stated that the head is just not a good place for this kind of prayer. And certainly the intellect is not a tool for contemplation. Neither are the emotions, imagination, memory nor any other faculties of the psyche. They may be creatively used in relational prayer. However, for the prayer of communion or identification, as Paul de Jaegher calls it, they are quite useless. Contemplation leads to an experience, the means of which are not accessible to the human psyche.

Are there any helps in the phenomenal world as preparation for contemplation? Certainly. Yamada Roshi always used to say that people coming to him from the art world seemed to have less trouble and come to *kensho* more quickly. I'm not sure that going out to start piano lessons as an adult will do the trick. But considering this point now in later life, I thought of the musical family I came from. Another entry in my Baby Book comes to mind.

> When Baby was just a little over three years old, I caught her up on top of the piano, plucking the strings of my violin. First she plucked the D string and then stopped and listened to its sound. Then she tried the A string. Surprisingly she didn't try to strum the 4 strings together. It was one at a time, and she seemed to listen to the different pitch and tonal differences of the various sounds. She seemed anxious to play like Bill and I play, so a short time later, I bought her a small violin and started lessons.

I have a vague memory of this, and very easily slipped into the routine of practice. Daily practice. Discipline. A fine pattern. I continue to follow this pattern even today. As I write this book, I follow a routine, sitting at the computer from 9 a.m. until 1 p.m. Then I leave it, until 9 a.m. the next day. Meditation takes a similar regard. Daily discipline. Priority. First thing. Until a year or so ago, I rose early each day, sometime between 5 and 6 a.m., and gave two hours to various kinds of prayer. But first, one hour of *zazen*.

It begins thus. Awaken naturally. A splash of water on the face. A full glass of water to drink. Striking the match for candlelight. Taking the incense. A slow and thoughtful *gassho*. Sitting on the front edge of the *zafu* (round sitting cushion). Bending the left leg. Knee on the *zabuton* (large cushion under the *zafu*). Lift right foot. Down on the left thigh. Straightening the backbone. Hands in position. Settling the spine. Lowering the eyes. Deep breath one. Exhale. Deep breath two. Exhale slowly. Deep breath three. Long exhalation. Then silence. Silence.

Making music begins in the body, too. Feel the shoulders. Flex the fingers. Take the instrument. Give it its shine. Tighten the bow. Get the feel of the bow on strings. Tune the strings. Adjust the shoulder pad. Loosen or tighten the bow tension just a fraction. Close the eyes. Breathe deeply once. Twice. Three times. A nod to the conductor and the most beautiful sounds in the world creep into Be-ing and flow back to Be-ing.

I read in a psychology book somewhere, sometime, that two of the highest joys in life are playing in a symphony orchestra and living within the radius of the smile of a person who loves you. I think of them today, my profession and my family, and a flood of memories dances around. I recall the psychologist used the word "galaxy," living life in the brilliant company of beauty and talent.

When I began work with prisoners many years later, I was to be grateful over and over again in my own youth for the presence of loving parents and siblings and home. I was grateful that there had been a program of activities and a routine to accomplish them. My brother and sisters and I all studied music and had to fulfill the requirement of 30 minutes of practice each day. Bill and I would get up early so that we could get out of doors, our first love. We were taught to respect time. My work with prisoners, almost all of whom had a miserable home life and upbringing, made me appreciate how important it is to have love and guidance at an early age. I long to embark on a program of help for inmates and their victims, and the families of both, even though the cause of their un-freedom is a multi-headed devil.

Zen, too, requires a family, a certain ambience, a good teacher and siblings who form the community of disciples called a *sangha*. Right from the beginning, some acknowledgment has to be given to the fact that there are very few true Zen teachers in the world today. Although Dogen Zenji has said it is better not to sit at all if one doesn't have a teacher, it is today often conceded that a beginner can sit according to written instructions, rather than not at all. Be that as it may, it is still an incontestable fact that once along the Way, one cannot do real Zen without a true teacher.

In all the Ways of the Orient, a deep bond develops between the master and disciple, and in Zen we even refer to our teacher in familial terms, such as "my father/mother in the dharma." The inside cover of each Kamakura Zendo magazine *Kyosho* (*The Awakening Bell*) contains this quotation from Dogen Zenji:

> It should be known that the subtle Dharma of the Seven Buddhas is maintained with its true significance when it is rightly transmitted to an enlightened disciple following an enlightened master. This is beyond the knowing of the priest of letter and learning.

This relationship is a living transmission, and when something living is transmitted, it is therefore not a doctrine or philosophy. It could, however, be said to have four characteristics:

1. Not relying on words or letters.

2. A direct and living transmission outside scriptures.

3. Pointing directly to the mind.

4. The key is to see into one's True Nature, which is to become an enlightened person.

Where is the starting point? After his great enlightenment, Shakyamuni spent the rest of his life, almost 50 years, teaching and guiding his disciples to realization. Buddhist scriptures recount only one disciple becoming fully enlightened, a certain Kasyapa. To him, Shakyamuni transmitted the "lamp of the Dharma." When truly enlightened teachers bring their disciples to an experience congruent with their own, and if the disciples demonstrate teaching ability, they are usually appointed Dharma successors. This is transmission. Following a period of seasoning, in Japan, the honorific title of *Roshi* (literally "old teacher") is usually bestowed.

When a *Roshi* and disciples who want to learn come together in practice, the group is called a *sangha* (Sanskrit for "community," connoting a kind of aliveness). As in the master– disciple relationship, the interaction amongst *sangha* members is of great significance. In Zen spirituality, *sangha* is not a noun, but a verb!

Perhaps it would be well for a moment here to consider the Christian parallel. Have you ever wondered what Christ meant when he said, "For where two or three are gathered in my name, I am there among them" (Matthew 18:20)? Of course we know that Divine Providence is always with us, whether we are alone or with others. It seems that Christ is saying that something extra is added, something special happens, when people pray together. Father de Mello always used to say that contemplation is practiced more fruitfully in a group than by oneself.

All sitters agree spontaneously that it is much easier to sit with a group. I suppose part of the explanation is the kind of experience we have all had of doing something with someone who does it well. A friend tells me that the eminent Canadian philosopher Bernard Lonergan claimed this is "method" in its purest form. For instance, how easy and even thrilling to sing between two vocalists! One is literally carried along and a special relatedness can evoke a bond between the two accompanists.

Something similar happens when we sit together in the *dojo* (place of practice). It is not uncommon in the Orient for a master to bring a struggling disciple to sit on the next cushion. If the unifying dynamism of *zazen* helps the individual to break down the sense of dualism and separateness, how much more easily will this be generated when there is an added dimension of two or more people who sit rather deeply in absorption. And one day, the interconnectedness grows to be mutually enriching.

Christianity in both its religion and various spiritualities has a strong tradition of relationships. Biblical scholars tell us God is an active verb. God's presence is life itself. It's not that the unifying dynamism comes and goes in its life-ing qualities. Hakuin Zenji's *Zazen Wasan* (*Song of Zazen*) tells us there is, for our Original Nature, no coming or going, and yet it is by always moving to and fro that one is always still. Vibrations are very real to a person sensitized by long hours of *zazen*. Sitting with others, whether more experienced than we are or not, is not only normally supportive, it could be the cause of our own growth and eventual realization.

John 14:20: "On that day you will know that I am in my Father, and you in me, and I in you."

When we leave our cushion each day, this generating power continues to move us in compassion and action. Zen spirituality is not just sitting. If we are plugged in, as it were, to the Source of power, we should be shot off our cushions for service in this world of greed, anger and ignorance. Thomas Aquinas says that the best of all lives is when activity flows from a superabundance of contemplation. The personal liberation that comes about through the emptying of oneself, one's selfishness and ego-centered orientation, is not the work of a moment, a few hours of sitting, or months, or even years. In Christian terms it is a work of grace, toward which we dispose ourselves in the practice of sitting, regulating our breathing, and attaining a point of focus.

Once beginners complete the first three or four months, they are usually aware that something is happening, no matter how fragile or tentative at first. If this were not so then we would have no Zen. It is too difficult a discipline in which to persevere, were there no dividends. The word I like to use in describing the process is "harmonizing." In sitting, this happens not only to the individual but to the group as well. This gift of community is best appreciated in fidelity and gratitude. Yamada Roshi would often stand among us in the Kamakura *zendo*, tasting that dynamism which bonds us. He would warn us not to be unmindful of it.

And that savoring is what Zen spirituality is about. It contains the definition of Zen I use most often: *Zen is experiencing fully at all times.* I am grateful that so much of my early life was of a quality that elicited such experiencing.

Chapter Seven

The Shared Sacred

(Isaiah 2:4)

When I first arrived in Kamakura, there was considerable discussion among the *Roshi's* disciples concerning a Theravadan monk who had come to Tokyo a short time before and performed astounding supra-normal feats. My memory of the occasion is that one of the monks under Harada Roshi, the virtual founder of the Sanbo Kyodan, attended a Zen session in a Tokyo hotel. The visitor from the south was speaking of the height (or was it depth?) of his concentration, and as proof, he predicted that he and the chair he was sitting on would rise to the ceiling and remain there for 55 minutes. This is precisely what he did. When the allotted time had passed, he and the chair slowly and safely descended to their original place. The visitor challenged all those present to show *their* degree of concentration. No one could do anything that spectacular.

The Sanbo Kyodan monk returned to his teacher crestfallen. Harada Roshi made short shrift of the problem. "Bah!" he exclaimed. "Who was he helping up there at the ceiling?" His monk then asked, "If you had been there, what would you have done?" Harada Roshi replied, "If I had been there, I would have said, 'I'm sure you're tired after that long trip. Here is a cup of tea to refresh you.'" And with the flowing movements that Zen Roshis often make, the famous teacher spread out his hands and mimed tea serving. The attending monk's head remained low and unconvinced. He remained enamoured of miracles. He still thought levitating is the way the Buddha Nature most fittingly revealed itself.

There is another startling story of a Zen Master, Ryutan by name. As he was dying, he lay on his bed moaning away his pain and agony. His attending monks were horrified that their revered Master was not enduring his death pangs with stoicism. Then the Zen Master taught them his last great lesson: "I am as much living the life of a Zen monk as when I sit in *zazen*. My death screams are the Buddha Nature just as surely as if I were chanting the sutras."

Although somewhat more user friendly now, Catholicism has in the past seen heroic virtue in stoicism. We do not expect our saints to die giving vociferous vent to their pain. I know I used to think that way. But the more I came to understand contemplative spirituality, the more I saw that such an expectation could come from an exalted opinion of the energy of spirit over matter. We tend to see the spirit of our inner nature as dominant. Indeed, we tend to see almost everything in relation to something else. Recently I read some words of Yamada Roshi where he is quoting a favourite old Zen worthy, Ganto: "When I stretch out my legs to sleep, there is neither falsehood nor truth." A fact is a fact, with nothing sticking to it.

After all, Christ said from the cross, "I thirst." Just that. In one of her books, Caryll Houselander says that she and some of her friends were able to accept Christianity in the end because of those words. I guess they never doubted Christ's divinity. It was evidently his humanity that confounded them and eventually won their allegiance.

In the most famous of all Zen chants, the Heart Sutra *Hannya Shingyo,* there is a marriage between the world that cannot be seen (Essential World) and the world that can be seen (phenomenal world). The chant goes: *shiki zoku ze ku, ku zoku ze shiki,* phenomena is nothing but Essential, Essential is nothing but phenomena. An applicable articulation of that would be, we find the world of the Spirit in the phenomenal, and we find the phenomenal in the spiritual world. When we come to live our life that way, we are in a real contemplative spirituality. Buddhists might point to their founding teacher's words, "There is an unborn, an un-originated, an unmade, an un-compounded. Were there not, oh mendicants, there would be no escape from the world of the born, the originated, the made and the compounded."

A buddha is one who has completed his or her personality. Or perhaps it is better to say, one whose personality has been completed. That is, the body is fully infused by the Buddha Nature, which gives life to the body without hindrance. Yamada Roshi once wrote in his magazine, *Kyosho:*

> Often I speak and write on how our essential self is empty while at the same time containing wondrous and ultimate capabilities. This is by no means just my personal opinion. I am convinced that this is the very essence of Zen. Zen is a world that cannot be perceived by the 5 senses. I do not speak in terms of mere nihilism, but rather of emptiness which contains infinite and wonderful capabilities. Among these marvellous capabilities I believe is the ability to heal the physical and spiritual disharmonies within us.

For me, the working of that inner Nature is Be-ing.

Apart from that perennial tug from the heart-mind, there is a wholeness and plenitude in our Be-ing (verb again) that gives attentive recognition to the physical. Because the body is so involved in sitting, people soon come to the personal experience that it is better to sit in the morning as soon as one awakens. Understanding that the intellect is at that time somewhat still, it is therefore in a helpful state for *zazen*. If the body and mind are not too exhausted before retiring in the evening, it is also beneficial to sit again at that time. Since sitting helps to quiet the psyche, sleep will be less dream-filled and more restful. However, many people have developed personal habits which make them day people while others are night people, and sitting times are perhaps best adjusted to these habits. In our *dojo* it was suggested that people sit two or three feet from a wall or curtain, with eyes open, but not actually trying to focus on seeing any one object.

Yamada Roshi succeeded admirably in maintaining his little *zendo* as a sacred place. Perhaps it would be more accurate to say he succeeded in getting his disciples to regard it as such and keep it sacred. For a year or so, I had charge of changing the water in the small cups on the three altars first thing in the morning, a ritual I regarded as a privilege. That precious commodity of water was first poured into plain, unadorned containers and with a bow, the fresh water was placed before the Buddha statue on the main altar, the Zen Masters' altar to the right, and the Yamada family altar to the left. On each altar, there was a small bell on which the *Roshi* sounded a "good morning." The Sacred is indeed shared; it seemed that I grew into that reality each day. As Teilhard de Chardin and Zen Masters tell us, there is no place that is secular for those who have the opened eye. This is not a facetious play on words. When they and the Bible speak about finally seeing with the opened eye, they all mean the same thing. In the Orient, we often refer to this kind of "seeing" as The Third Eye.

In any case, we do our *zazen* in a place set aside for sitting, in an area which is clean and tidy and away from jarring noises, particularly those of the human voice. Natural sounds like birds or running water or the ticking of a clock can be very helpful for *zazen*. How well I remember the *Roshi*'s assistant settling us down early one day in *sesshin* with the words "*Saiwai ni, ame ga futte imasu*" (You are blessed, it is raining). Natural sounds are the best notes struck on the road into the world of silence.

Gassho (bringing the palms of the hands together) was also something that conveys a sense of the hallowed. Bowing and incense and flowers and lighted candles tend to keep our senses open. We were taught to sit in subdued lighting and coolish temperature, if possible, and counselled to wear clean and comfortable clothing. *Zendo* regulations call for inconspicuous, nonfigured clothes with a high neckline. *Dojos* tend to be meticulous about dress. Each of the martial arts, for example, has its own distinctive garb.

Despite many stories to the contrary, I found that the Zen Way is not asceticism. There is certainly no coddling in a good *zendo*, but a wise master is not unmindful of the harmful effects of Shakyamuni's excessive self-denial. I remember when I was given permission to make a kind of private *sesshin* under the severe leadership of Fukagai Roshi at Enkoji. She indicated the little cottage on the temple grounds I was to have, produced the proposed schedule, and then thrust a bag of cookies in front of me, saying, "Here – in case you get hungry. We might forget at times to leave your meal on the doorstep, and you can't sit on an empty stomach." The bottom line in sitting is to forget oneself and become one with the practice. At first we are all a bit self-conscious, but in time it is like hopping into a car and becoming one with it. *Zazen* is simple, really. It is nothing sophisticated or esoteric, as some would have us believe. It is not even very interesting, but the daily feedback and the determination to attain the goal bolster perseverance. It is almost always surprising to find that the discipline of some kind of breath concentration (there are various breathing practices) is so simple and yet so difficult. Not only that, it is a simplicity that admits of no variety, no excitement, and no thought content with which to keep your mind entertained.

I never thought of myself as a hermitage dweller, but the practice apparently developed that capacity. Be-ing, while alone in the world of silence, *is* a hermitage. Halfway through the 1990s, a friend from Singapore bought an apartment in Oxford and rented it to me at a price I could afford. For three years, I was a hermit in one sense and never alone in another. I finally got to the point where I experienced the commonality of the Sacred. This came when I seemed to be given a way to practice emptying, accomplished by silencing the mind. On the wall of the Oxford apartment was a large painting by Turner that glowed with light. IT filled the whole canvas. Turner painted the sacred as light, emulating the words of the northern poet James Thomson, "illumined with fluid gold."

It was in that hermitage apartment that I started to realize that *I*, so to speak, was a verb. Or, as my editor says, I strive to live "in a continuous present tense." Living became life-ing; eating became eat-ing; being sick was just retch-ing. At first, this "ing-ing" may seem to some to be a practice in awareness, and somewhat artificial. But gradually, one comes to live in the present moment and at the present place by Be-ing in a very natural way. In so many *teisho*, Yamada Roshi used to say washing dishes is just washing dishes, not to get them done, but just to wash dishes. I try to show this by verb-ing it; just wash-ing dishes, just stand-ing up, just sitt-ing down, just drink-ing tea, when done in the continuous present or Being present, are all practices. An *ikebana* arrangement never ceases to live this way. A well-executed *jijitsu* is presenting the shared Sacred. So does one of our sisters as she sets the table.

To live out this Be-ing process is to do only one thing at a time. How fractured we become when we do two or three things simultaneously. I recall I used to iron, listen to the radio, and plan the following week's work all at the same time. It never dawned on me why I never liked ironing and why I was such a poor ironer! But when I learned to let Be-ing be, then I didn't require capital letters any longer. The Sacred became as precious and as common as water.

When touching on this point of awareness in *teisho*, Yamada Roshi would sometimes point to Larry McGarrell, Jesuit pianist and disciple. "Have you ever noticed how he gathers all his forces into unity when he plays the piano? As he leans over the keyboard, his whole being is directed toward the music: his body, his mind, his emotions, his everything." I suggest to my disciples that they check themselves occasionally during the day, as do I. Not *how* we are doing something, but just the fact that we are doing it, the living fact! But awareness will gradually mature into openness, boundaries become indistinct, and we are closer to living the Reality of life.

Away from our cushion, Zen spirituality is redirecting wandering thoughts, and this discipline gradually makes us alive to the moment. It is a spirituality of very ordinary everyday life, but *experiencing* as we live our life. How mighty, clean and pure it is just to sit, just to walk, just to eat. This is, in Oriental spirituality, to be alive.

What a delight to find in St. Paul a hint of a parallel. In 1 Corinthians 10:31, Paul tells us that everything we do is for the glory of God, and when he gives a couple of examples, he does not mention praying, freeing prisoners, or visiting the sick, or even social justice, although these obviously are appropriate venues for the marketplace. Paul mentions eating and drinking.

The here and now is our place and time of practice. It is all we really have. In the Zen experience, the Buddha learned that this is not depletion, but a participation in fullness which is "not yet." And in this reality all is present, in both past and future.

I left Japan in 1976 with the prospect of sitting alone for an indefinite period. Yamada Roshi wrote a farewell message in his magnificent flowing calligraphy: *Za ga aru toki, tsune ni, waga iru.* (Whenever you sit, without fail, I will be sitting with you.) He likened my adventure of introducing Zen in the Philippines to the arrival of the first great Patriarch Bodhidharma in China. In biography, it is almost impossible to separate fact from fiction, but it is commonly recounted that after Bodhidharma reached China, this famous missioner sat alone for nine years before his first disciple, Eka, appeared.

I am reminded of an incident which transpired one evening just before I left Japan. I was having supper with the Yamadas, and the *Roshi's* wife and I were chatting. Several times she said something to the effect that I would be the first to go and live in the Philippines to teach Zen. "You'll be just like Bodhidharma!" she exclaimed. Remembering his first nine years of sitting alone, I said, "I wonder how long it will be before Eka comes." At this, the *Roshi* drew himself up to his full stature and looked at me gravely. "I don't think your concern is about Eka, but whether or not Bodhidharma will be there!"

Buddhas and Bodhisattvas and Patriarchs have kept the lamp burning from Shakyamuni and Bodhidharma right down to our present day. By the year 1000, there were many Japanese Buddhist monks making the then-perilous journey to China to study at the feet of the famous masters. Great names come to mind, including Dogen Zenji, whom Thomas Merton called his kindred spirit. I find him my greatest teacher among the old Zen worthies.

Dogen brought Soto Zen back to Japan, and his name and presence are revered in all the Sanbo Kyodan *Zendos* today. He was unappreciated for hundreds of years because his teachings were misunderstood. I have often paralleled his life with that of Thomas Aquinas. They were both of noble birth, with an early call to a religious vocation, and both men had a superlative intellect. Their voluminous written works were misunderstood for hundreds of years and only recently exposed to light and recognition. Eventually both these intellectuals sought the Transcendent in actual experience.

Dogen was born in Kyoto on January 2, 1200, within the court circle of the day. His father, a descendant of the emperor Murakami, died when Dogen was only two years old. Dogen was raised in an over-refined cultural atmosphere, and educated in the Japanese and Chinese classics, which he studied enthusiastically. He was also trained in literary skills and techniques, which made him sensitive to language. In this vein he wrote an instruction entitled *Ago* (Loving Speech). Dogen's mother was Motofusa, the daughter of the prominent Fujiwara family; she died when he was seven years old. Before her death, she earnestly requested Dogen to seek the truth by becoming a monk, which offered him the kind of life where he could help relieve the tragic sufferings of humanity. Motofusa's death was a serious blow to Dogen's fragile and sensitive mind. In the midst of his grief, Dogen later said that he experienced the impermanence of all things as he watched the incense ascending at his mother's funeral service.

When he was 12, and mindful of his mother's exhortation, he decided to become a monk. He was ordained in 1213 at Enryakuji Temple, right up on *my* Mount Hiei, as I very soon got to regard the famous mountain after I arrived in Kyoto.

He did a systematic study of the *sutras*. No more favorable educational environment could be found in his day than on Mount Hiei. It is said that Dogen devoured these studies with his gifted mind. On February 22, 1223, he set out for China.

Dogen found the teaching uneven at the various temples he went to see. For some time he lived aboard the vessel on which he had sailed, and visited many of the teachers by taking excursions from his floating home. Strangely enough, he was most impressed by a Zen monk who came to the ship to buy *shitake*, Japanese mushrooms. The monk was the *tenzo* (cook) of his monastery, and Dogen found his answers to questions very satisfying. Early in their relationship, Dogen tried to engage the cook in long conversation, but the *tenzo* was in a hurry to return to his kitchen. Dogen chided him that *anyone* can cook, and it would be better for him to stay on the ship a while longer. The cook replied that cooking was his practice and no one could do it for him. Dogen learned much from this *tenzo* and later was ashamed of his attitude. He decided to go to the temple to meet the monk's teacher.

It was on May 1, 1225, that Dogen met Ju-ching, the Chinese Zen Master who was to become his most important teacher. This man proved a warm and loving father to the young Japanese. He made himself available to Dogen, and this availability rekindled the young man's inquiring mind with a burning desire for truth. Dogen was later to say, "If you don't meet the right master, it is better not to study Zen at all." Thereafter he held to the absolute necessity of having a personal encounter in Zen practice with a teacher.

Once after night *zazen* during *ango* (a 100-day period of intensive practice) in 1225, Dogen heard his teacher saying, "*Zazen* is the falling away of body and mind." Dogen, hearing this, suddenly experienced deep enlightenment. He went up to the Master's room, lit an incense stick, and prostrated himself in a deep bow. When his teacher asked why he had performed that ritual, Dogen replied, "I have come here, having body and mind fallen away." After examining the experience, his teacher was later to say, "It is no small thing for a foreigner to attain to this degree."

Dogen lived in the early half of the Kamakura period (1192–1333), at a time when radical changes in society were underway in Japan. The country was burdened with imitating the political and social pattern of the Tang Dynasty in China. Eventually, it shook itself free from the troublesome formalism of its aristocratic government and then moved to a military one. Interest in Buddhism was flourishing, and among the connoisseurs, it was well known that the brilliant Dogen had gone to China to study. It is said that when he returned to Japan, there was a large crowd to greet him, inquiring about the changes he had undergone as a direct result of his new knowledge. Dogen is reported to have said, "My eyes are still horizontal, my nose is still vertical, and there is not a smell of Buddhism about me." The Sanbo Kyodan stream of Zen has always endeavored to maintain this lack of external opulence and showmanship.

Often when visitors come, I have to account for the fact that I do not have a plethora of Buddhist statues around. I do have one photo of the Bodhisattva Miroku, found in the Kitano Shrine in Kyoto. My reticence extends to images of Christ as well. I have one photo of a crucifix taken in a small chapel on one of the Arran islands off the west coast of Ireland. It dates back to the fifth or sixth century, and I find its Celtic antiquity very appealing. The presence of both of these photos comforts me as representations of the religious world. But it is Turner's painting *Norham Castle,* bristling with light and life, that beckons the intuition. It would engage me the minute I entered the flat. And I used to think a hermit loved being alone!

Traditional Buddhism was a religion for noblemen, and had degenerated into a kind of esoteric practice or collection of magical rites. In contrast to this, the Buddhism of Dogen's era celebrated a return to simply understood fundamentals. Zen was one of the three main sects central to this new Buddhism.

Dogen's Soto Zen accentuated *zazen* more than anything else. Among the abundance of teachings available at that time, Dogen's show the strongest tendency to return to the original true spirit of Shakyamuni, where an appeal is made to fluid and direct intuition, rather than static and rigid logic. A person arrives at wisdom, not as a result of logical reasoning, but through enlightenment experiences which, however, do not negate the intellect. Dogen does not ignore the need for the mind to be continually refined through sitting. He teaches that in this process, the mind returns to its pure, original spontaneity, and it will always be able to exercise this wisdom appropriately. "Assisting the mind to return to its original state is of the essence of *zazen*," he reminds us. We do *shikantaza* by be-ing our breath.

In particular, Dogen advocated *shikantaza* (just sitting). It is pure *zazen*, no counting, no following the breath, no thinking or remembering or feeling or picturing. Just sitting. Simplicity. Silent body, silent mind and silent ego brings about a state where the Sacred is given leave to take over, and lives its own life. The literal meaning of the word *shikantaza* is "strong." *Shi* means "only, just, solely, exclusively, single-mindedly"; it is the character that is read *tada* ("just" or "only" in Japanese). The combination with *kan,* which literally means "tube," makes the compound readable as *hitasure* (earnestly). *Ta* is "hit" and *za* is "seat." So, hit the seat earnestly, single-mindedly, would be the literal translation of *shikantaza*.

There are exaggerated representations of *shikantaza* in some books. Perhaps these practitioners are hitting the seat rather too forcefully. I do not advocate this to my disciples. There are times in prolonged sitting when the process itself seems to take over, everything becomes easy, and there is no longer pain in the legs, or a need to take a deep breath and start all over. One seems to be suspended in a happy no man's land, perfectly calm and still, and usually unaware of the passage of time but nevertheless responding to all the bells and the change of action they signify. We call this state *samadhi* (Sanskrit: intense yet effortless meditation).

In a Kamakura *sesshin* there is a long period of sitting from 1:30 until 4:30 each afternoon. I remember sitting beside Fr. Lassalle in one *sesshin*, and I knew he was in *samadhi* all the afternoon. How? Because for one thing, his movements when we were doing *kinhin* (walking meditation) were the tiniest bit freer than usual. The same thing has been said of me at times. There seems only one word that covers what happens during *samadhi*, and that is the verb "to be." I tend to want to capitalize it. And that kind of sitting, I tend to call Be-ing. Total silence but still the highest activity on earth and in the heavens. It is not only a method of self-help, but eminently vicarious. It can be brought into everyday life. Here I find that I want to rewrite the first sentence in this book, "I was be-ing one with the sand, one with the sea. . . ." It has taken years to develop this ability to tap into the Great Source and bring IT (that Great source which cannot be named) into play. On the other hand, it is as common as water, and even more plentiful, and there is no need at all to write in capital letters, since it is the essence all of creation shares.

Speaking as a Christian, I have always thought that *shikantaza* is perfect contemplation. I have often defined Christian contemplation as allowing the Holy Spirit to spin

Its cocoon within, and then allow IT to move out to the 10,000 things in the phenomenal world and interact with them appropriately. This activity is called "love"; hence the depth of realization in John of the Cross's aphorism "Love is my only destiny."

Dogen's *Fukanzazengi* is his manifesto of Soto Zen for Japan, in which he explains *shikantaza* as a practice of sitting by which the mind is set free, and returned to the state of its activity as a pure liberated spirit. If the student wants this inner spirit to be always acting appropriately, the practice of *zazen* must be continued without interruption. Dogen taught that enlightenment is always concerned with the practice.

Such simplicity can be easily misconstrued. Over the centuries, Dogen's great erudition, his concern for people and society, and his religious stature have sometimes been reduced to quips, and even in contemporary Japan, Soto monks can be heard preaching that Dogen had no use for *satori*, and that *dokusan* and *teisho* are of no value since it suffices only to sit. Fortunately, in the last century, Dogen's true teaching has reappeared, and more and more today, his difficult works are slowly being unravelled and understood.

Many Asian countries have helped to form Zen as it is today. Indian Zen is considered to have been philosophical, but it never filtered down to common people and didn't last more than about a thousand years. Zen's journey in the fifth or sixth century CE into the earthy and poetic hands of the Chinese certainly changed considerably in its encounter with Taoism and Confucianism. Its transfer to Japan saw fewer changes because the Japanese, with their innate sense of excellence, were loath to tamper with this precious jewel. They did, however, give of their own genius, and Zen took on new life and vigor in the hands of the pragmatic Japanese.

In this 21st century, Zen continues its journey into different cultures and religions. In North America, the Zen path was started by two great teachers, Shibayama Zenkei Roshi and Yasutani Hakuun Roshi. In the early 1960s, when I first became interested in studying Zen in Japan, Father Hugo Enomiya-Lassalle guided me to the Rinzai nuns, where I met a young nun named Tadama Kodo San. She took me to their principal *dojo*, Enkoji, in north Kyoto, where Fukagai Roshi taught. Its male counterpart is the famous Nanzenji, where Shibayama Roshi was teaching at the time. It was Fukagai Roshi's custom not to give *teisho* during *sesshin*. Instead, we all walked daily to Nanzenji to hear Shibayama Roshi. The residents of north Kyoto were frequently alerted to my appearance as I, a lone straggler wearing black and a succession of scarves and wraps, brought up the rear of an impressive line of neatly dressed Buddhist nuns walking single file through the residential district en route to Nanzenji. The deep cold in all the Japanese *zendos* accounted for my haphazard appearance.

I never felt at home in the Rinzai harshness of Enkoji, but the thrusts in Shibayama's fine *teisho* were the catalysts I needed to stay, and account for the long period of time I spent in Rinzai Zen. Shibayama Roshi journeyed to the United States, pointing to Zen's ubiquitous gateless gate, but his successors are caught up in the busy-ness of running Nanzenji, and it seems they do not have an overseas apostolate.

Yasutani Roshi, in the Soto-based Sanbo Kyodan, made several trips to North America and Europe before he died in March 1973, leaving Yamada Koun Roshi, my teacher, as his chief successor. So it fell into my teacher's capable hands to found and build Sanbo Kyodan Zen centers in so many other cultures and religions.

At about the same time that these Japanese Zen teachers moved outward, a momentous event was happening in Christendom. In the mid-1960s, under the aegis of the beloved Pope John XXIII, the Catholic Church embarked on a renewal resulting from an assembly of all the bishops throughout the world at the second Vatican Council. One of the Council documents, *Ad Gentes* (To the Gentiles), influenced me greatly. It gave credence to my journeying, and brought out articulations of indigenous Oriental spirituality. The document told Christians and the world that we hold in deep respect all the great religions, for they contain "those seeds which God's own hand has planted in our ancient cultures even before the Gospel was preached to our people." Another document spoke about different rays of truth that God has entrusted to each of the great religions for which we must search if we are to know more of the full grandeur of the Infinite.

The message of Vatican II was reiterated with even more clarity in the Asian Bishops' Second Plenary Assembly, held in Bangalore, India, in 1978. In their message, the Asian bishops wrote:

> We are daily more convinced that the Spirit is leading us in our time, not to some dubious syncretism (which we all rightly reject) but to an integration, profound and organic in character, of all that is best in our Asian and traditional forms of prayer and worship, into the treasury of our Christian heritage. Thus is a fuller catholicity made possible in this age of the Church.

> Asian prayer has much also to offer to authentic Christian spirituality; a richly-developed prayer of the whole person, in unity of body-psyche-spirit; contemplation of deep interiority and immanence; venerable books and writings; traditions of asceticism and renunciation; techniques of contemplation found in the ancient Eastern religions; simplified prayer forms and other popular expressions of faith and piety.

And there was more.

The [Asian] Church seeks to share in whatever truly belongs to the culture of our people . . . and this involves a living dialogue with the great religions of Buddhism, Hinduism and Islam . . . over many centuries, they have been a treasury of many of the religious experiences of our ancestors from which our contemporaries do not cease to draw light and strength.

The best means to assimilate the riches of Eastern religious values, and one of the most important ways to contemplation, are in the traditions of ashrams. This will be a specific contribution of Asia to the treasury of the life of humanity at this stage in the growth of the Church.

The techniques developed in Asian religious traditions, such as yoga and zen, are of great service to the prayer experience of immanence. The spirituality of immanence can lead us to newer insights into theology. It can further help us discover an Asian spirituality for Christians.

The real encounter between the Church and our ancient religious traditions will take place at the deeper level of contemplative experiences. Hence the need for the inculturation of prayer of Asian Christians, in keeping with the economy of incarnation which is the law of the Church's life and mission.

In the wake of such hopeful signs, at the invitation of the Church, I started teaching Zen in the Philippines. After several years of carrying our own cushions back and forth, we celebrated our 10th anniversary of foundation, with Cardinal Sin officiating at the opening of our small new meditation hall in the Marikina district of Manila. The well-known Jesuit, Fr. William Johnston, author of many books on Eastern and Western mysticism, was to call this event "epoch-making." Describing the opening and blessing of the Zen Center in Manila on February 24, 1984, Johnston wrote:

I have been in Japan over 30 years, and have seen the few, like Sister Elaine, who persevered through the long Zen training exacted by a true Master, and I have wondered and felt that it will be a hundred years before we know what the Church will do with Zen. And yet, here we see Sister Elaine guiding a group of people through legitimate Zen for almost 10 years. When they finally celebrated the gift of a home, the head of the institutional church and Asia's leading theologian confirm her work with their presence. I never thought that could possibly happen within my lifetime. It is truly epoch-making!

(*Scarboro Mission Magazine*, 1985)

Present-day realities in the inter-religious dialogue continue in much the same trend. It would be too extensive an endeavor here to list the interaction among all the different religions, but I should like to mention the growing interest almost everywhere in the Oriental understanding of the human being.

Zendos seem to be springing up everywhere, but alas, the majority flounder, as they bypass the real thing. Many people today seem content to have a group to sit with, and give their own assessment of their spiritual maturing. It is almost commonplace for people to tell me how many *kensho* experiences they have had. Indeed, one priest said he has one every day. So there!

With my transfer to the Philippines in 1976, Yamada Roshi approved the opening of the Manila Zen Center, and one month after arriving in Manila, I was asked by the country's leading theologian to start a Zen center for the Filipino Church. In 1985, Cardinal Sin officiated at the opening of our newly purchased *zendo* in Quezon City. When people ask me about the factors involved in placing Zen in the hands of Christians, I not only relate the above, but also unfailingly mourn the name of my revered teacher, Yamada Koun Roshi. The moment he welcomed new disciples who were Christian, the *Roshi* made it clear that he would help them become better Christians. This transpires not only in the process that sitting is, but also in the Zen experience of *kensho*, to which this great man brought many of his Christian disciples.

Yamada Koun Roshi was freed to do this by the depth of his own experience. He had several sisters, priests, seminarians and committed lay Christians among his disciples; to them he brought new appreciation of their Christian faith. As he explained many times, he would not have it otherwise. He did wonder why so many Christians whose religious faith had for centuries been rich with teachers in contemplative prayer came to him for guidance in prayer, and he chided those of us whom he allowed to teach to give seekers a shot in the arm, as far as contemplative prayer is concerned. But he had the highest regard for the Church. He was convinced that the lamp of illumination, the transmission in the line of the great Buddhas and Bodhisattvas and Patriarchs, is the transmission of the true experience of enlightenment. He felt that since it was in the field of religious experience and not doctrine, Zen could be absorbed by all the world's great religions. "How you articulate that experience within the framework of your own religion is your responsibility," he used to tell us.

During these years, the *Roshi* himself grew in appreciation of Christianity, and he often referred to that giant of a missionary, Fr. Hugo Enomiya-Lassalle S.J., as his ideal human being. Conversely, in a private chat I had with Fr. Lassalle one day, he predicted that Yamada Roshi would one day be recognized as one of the greatest Zen masters of our age, because of the gigantic bridge he had started building between Buddhist Zen and the rest of the world.

These two leaders died within months of each other, and at a memorial service for Fr. Lassalle held in the Tokyo Cathedral, Mrs. Yamada was invited to speak. She vividly recounted the intimate relationship that had developed between her husband and the famous Jesuit. She ended by saying, "I'm sure they're together somewhere right now, discussing the points of convergence between Zen and Christianity." Let us hope the day will soon dawn when the same relationship can be said to exist amongst the peoples of all religions. Since practicing Zen breaks down the sense of supposed separation between the self and others, it is superlative material for the bridge needed in inter-religious dialogue.

Zen orientation would have us be mindful that we never sit alone. The whole family of creation sits with us. Perhaps no one has pictured this serene reality more graphically than Isaiah 11:6-9.

> The wolf shall live with the lamb,
> the leopard shall lie down with the kid,
> the calf and the lion and the fatling together,
> and a little child shall lead them.
> The cow and the bear shall graze,
> their young shall lie down together;
> and the lion shall eat straw like the ox.
> The nursing child shall play over the hole of the asp,
> and the weaned child shall puts its hand
> on the adder's den.
> They will not hurt or destroy
> on all my holy mountain;
> for the earth will be full of the knowledge of the LORD
> as the waters cover the sea.

What a reminder Isaiah sheds on the potential of our ecological reality. I was absolutely delighted to read David Suzuki's superlative book *The Sacred Balance: Discovering Our Place in Nature.* What is true for the phenomenal aspect of each human being is true for each particle of creation.

Suzuki points out that the first two human beings in the Bible are named Adam, from the Hebrew *adama*, meaning "earth" or "soil," and Eve, from *hava*, meaning "living." As David

Suzuki asserts, together they make the eternal connections: earth comes from life, and the earth is *alive*. He points out several creation stories which also deal with the same material, proving in the end we human beings are *earthenware!*

Life comes from the earth. Our own native peoples have shared this truth with their counterparts all over the universe. One articulation of this simple truth appeals to me enormously: "We are alive as much as we keep the earth alive."

I was to learn further from this excellent book that to be born by the sea is concomitant with "to be born of the sea." Even for the earth, the sea was where it all was born. In the early life of earth, it was too hot for water to exist in its liquid form. Gradually the atmosphere cooled and water was able to condense into clouds. Eventually those clouds were able to release their content, on the rocks below. As it rained, water collected in every depression, filling each one, which then flowed down to the next containment. Pulled by gravity, water overflowed, and the depressions became creeks and rivers, dragging rocks along, scouring out channels, and always running to a lower level. Tiny one-celled creatures cleaned the waters, added oxygen to the air, made food and energy from the sun. After millions of years, fresh water covered most of the earth. These tiny creatures made the way for all else that was to be. Each new form of life-power unfolding ever more complex and diverse, bearing in itself the wisdom that went before. Plants swept ashore and lured animals to follow. Giant green forests filled with life, glaciers formed and moved around, and then all else tumbled forth.

While in the Philippines, I gradually became conscious that the earth, too, had its own spirituality. At precisely that point, a young man, Nicanor Perlas, returned home after many years of study abroad and introduced in a practical manner Rudolf Steiner's teaching on the subject of agriculture. It was called "biodynamic farming" – *bio* meaning life, and *dyames* meaning forces. Nicky called his course "a production education approach with a human face," and taught both scientific theories and practical skills, and the human and cultural dimensions of farming. What a revelation it proved to be! Actually meeting the dynamic life-ing in the earth, which longs to have its potential realized by encouraging the interaction of specific natural elements. Using this technique, we saw the tired Manila soil produce large, beautiful, delicious and nutritious vegetables. Wearing knee-high rubber boots, we sloshed through the mud, learned the practical skills of seedflat management, bed preparation, composting, transplanting, watering, weeding, multiple cropping, pest control, harvesting, storage, green manuring, basic agro-eco-systems design, farm planting and innovative methods of scientific observation. We even divined for water. It was a glorious time and thrilling to discover that some of the agricultural methods used in the biodynamic procedures are identical to those of the mountain people in Northern Luzon whose secrets were thousands of years old. The Sacred is shared!

The course that caught my interest was composting. We cleared a piece of ground a meter and a half square, and then made several layers of twigs, grass, leaves, earth, prepared water (using the five biodynamic preparations), until the mound was about a meter and a half high. Then we poked a hole in each corner and the center by means of a long pole. Into these we inserted a small amount of the five biodynamic preparations made from such ordinary sources as dandelions, stinging nettle and bark of the valerian tree. Then we gave the whole pile another good watering, and covered it with a large piece of plastic. At the end of 30 days, we lifted the cover. Voilà! There was a wonderful pile of clean-smelling compost, with its life forces all set to go into action.

Steiner based his work on the need for nutrition. He did so in a philosophical way. In his series of eight famous lectures on agriculture, Steiner stated that the most energizing and inspiring of our human capacities is the possibility of changing an idea into an ideal. We have to be able to muster the strength to do so. He preached that food plants no longer contain the forces people need for this work. He said this in 1924, long before the day when processed, refined and preserved foods would provide the questionable diet for so many of our people as they do today.

In this area of his teaching, Nicky used the word *aletheia*, the gradual unfolding of truth in the human consciousness. This is very evident in physics today where we are moving beyond the mechanistic and into the quantum approach. In agriculture, Steiner saw that some traditional practices and knowledge handed down from past understanding of nature were losing their value. He said, "Humanity has no other choice. Either we must learn once more, in all domains of life . . . learn from the whole nexus of Nature and the Universe . . . or else we must see Nature and with it the life of Man himself degenerate." As early as the 1920s, he saw the question of nutrition, both for human beings and animals, requiring a *new learning*.

Now at the turn of the century, not only Britain but the whole world is in the midst of an agricultural crisis. Perhaps we are more ready to look at the food we eat. It is said that in our present "scientific" frame of mind, we have forgotten that our nourishment comes from *living* plants and animals. This life-force remains bound to the substance of the food for a time, then it withdraws and the food decomposes. Many methods have been employed to mask this withdrawal of life-forces from the substance, to preserve the form, flavor and aroma of the original food. Yet it is the very life-forces in the food we eat that give us our vitality.

If as early as 1924 the plant life of the Earth was losing its vitality, is there anything we can do now to reverse the direction? The answer is *yes,* but it demands that we embark upon this new path of learning from Nature once again. Rudolf Steiner points out that the plant is entirely embedded in the rhythmic life of the cosmos. To help bring vitality back into Nature, we must be willing to expand our range of concepts, to include a world of real life-forces. Knowledge of these forces (or ethers) was common in the past, but as humanity lost its awareness of all but the material world, talk of the ethers became a vague mystical allusion to something beyond the physical. It is the adverse effect of our propensity to separate and divide, especially in our thinking process. The discipline of a spiritual science which takes life-forces into account can bring to humanity the new health-bearing insights and techniques which are so desperately needed.

In agriculture this applies most directly to the soil itself as it shares the sacred with us. The solid–earth can bear the life principle or not. We try as farmers to preserve the life in our manures and decaying plant material, and hold it in the soil to support the life of future plants. By careful composting and handling of manures, the fertility of land can be built up over the years. Food plants grown on "living soil" are then more alive in themselves, and hardier.

A sad contrast to this approach is found in modern agricultural techniques such as hydroponic methods, which do away with the soil altogether. Nutrients are added from the mineral realm through chemicals, rather than in remaining in the cycles of life. Plants raised this way are weak and vulnerable. More and more death surrounds the ever-weakening life of these plants. Steiner claims the same story can be told of animal husbandry.

Biodynamic farming taught me not only the value of life itself and living it (dare I say life-ing it) but also educating farmers and gardeners concerning the observation of and respect for life-processes that can turn the tide. And we who have been raised on cheap food and bargain consciousness will have to revalue our priorities and support our farmers in the transition to new methods. We used to have a system of agriculture that relied on the farmer's instinct and the public's trust. Now it is replaced by the demands of an aggressive and manipulative food industry, fuelled by greed, encouraged by unproved science, allowed by ignorant governments and, by default, given the seal of approval by us, the consumers. The healing of the Earth itself is at stake. We are challenged to read the book of nature anew, behold its secrets, and become responsible for its renewal.

Chapter Eight

Swords into Ploughshares

I've read it a thousand times, but it continues to jolt. John of the Cross, whose very name suggests suffering and privation, has posited: Love is my only destiny. Now I can understand that pithy saying to be the quintessence of a life well lived, a belief that could be true for us all. When we have a retreat day, I sometimes check myself. "Can I answer that challenge honestly? How much have I grown from my teenage understanding of destiny? Is love a free upsurging from my deepest being?"

One surprising teaching I received from Yamada Roshi was that virtue should come from within. He saw no growth or maturity evolving when we are *told* to do something. He never asked us, his disciples, to do anything. We had to volunteer. Even that could be ego-driven, but at least the impulse came from us, whatever the motive. I noticed in myself that if I volunteered to do something because it should be done, then the energizing juice ran short rather quickly: almost totally if I had to do the job alone. It wasn't until I was well along in *koan* study that I could honestly say it didn't make any difference if someone else appraised what I was doing or not. The tradition in our *dojo* was to keep beginners on the same practice until their first *kensho* experience, and then they moved on to the study of the many and various *koans*. Until that point, we tended to be sword carriers, ready to go to battle at the least provocation. Sword carriers! Many people early in their spiritual quest argue, confront or take issue with just about anything, which turns lives into a series of battles. This is a recipe for unhappiness and frustration. Without a doubt we do have conflicts, but let us choose them wisely, otherwise we become victims, under the incessant demands of our equalizing ego.

The currently popular book title says, Don't Sweat the Small Stuff. Undoubtedly this is good psychology, and helpful advice when we're in the do-it-yourself, sword-carrying stage. Zen does not treat anything as small stuff, and sitting melts the swords and helps us shape them into ploughshares. That is the blueprint for each and every journeyer.

A woman I have known for years died recently. My thoughts continue to turn to her life story. Death is certainly one of the most sensitizing experiences life has to offer. I saw her rather often when her family was young and glowing and attractive. She bragged about the children then, said she had a good thing going, and they all filled a pew in the church they attended each Sunday morning. She was an environmentalist, and did much speaking and writing about this most sensitive need. For a while the world was at her doorstep. She was held in high respect, and life seemed to go well.

Then all of a sudden things went wrong. She lost her job and seemed to see herself only as a failure, while outwardly denying this. She took it out on the family and the community, became something of an alcoholic and was gradually forced to live alone, becoming quite eccentric and unyielding. Although the family visited her as her health deteriorated, she died alone.

What happens when a human being, full of potential, does battle with life, and is not able to relinquish aggression? It is a cause for tears. It seems no one ever told her, as Sogyal Rinpoche said so many times, that meditation is the most wonderful gift she could have given herself.

Tears are the subject of many Zen stories. Perhaps the most famous one concerns a grandmother whose favorite grandchild had died. She was inconsolable. Her friends chided her that being the zealous Zen person she was would surely shield her from sorrow and tears. She replied that the very stones would cry out if she did not weep. Another story mentions a woman in distress over the death of her son who came to the Master for comfort. He listened to her patiently while she poured out her tale of woe. Then he said softly, "I cannot wipe away your tears, my dear. I can only tell you that they are holy."

I think the reason I chose to spend the last active years of my life trying to help people who are experiencing failure is that it is such fertile soil for despair to those already on a downward spiral. I find that prisoners often feel their failures in their family relationships, in school, in sports, and often even in their criminality. In the early years of their incarceration, they almost always deny their crime. The prisoners who meditate, though, seem at some point, perhaps as many as five years later, to come to the point where they can say, "I did it." Usually after that there is some hope for change for the better. Being in denial never helps growth. The sword remains a sword.

Was I a sword carrier in my early years? Yes, I loved causes. I think my music added juice to youthful ardor. There are those familiar with the Enneagram who would say a number Seven is not someone who picks fights and heads for the fray.

Maybe not, but the upside of our personality is that we are enthusiasts. Look out when we're on fire!

I think we enthusiasts start to grow up when we realize that we can't know everything. We sooner or later get used to that fact, and not knowing is okay! One point which tickles me in Dr. Carlson's book urges that we not attempt to see life as fair. He says, "Life isn't fair ... it's a bummer ... but absolutely true ... one of the mistakes many of us make is that we think it should be fair ... well, it isn't and it won't be." Let's take another viewpoint.

I can truly say that the sword-carrying prisoners I have dealt with did not chant the life-is-not-fair mantra, even though they might have had every reason to think that was so. Most of the young offenders I met have come from dysfunctional families from whom they felt they had to flee. On the streets they met with companionship and lived by stealth. They knew they would eventually be picked up and put inside, during which painful time instinct reigned. Once inside, it was a matter of survival, which usually resulted in collecting a few more aggressive techniques. And then one day, they would perhaps see, for what seemed the first time, the poster on the wing bulletin board, a parachutist free-flying over mountain tops, and the caption WHOEVER THOUGHT FREEDOM COULD BE FOUND IN PRISON! Signed by the Prison Phoenix Trust.

Ordinarily, we Oriental meditation teachers never advertise. This tradition is built on the trust that when a disciple needs it, a teacher will appear. I never fully understood what made prisoners, whose point of view is usually from the bottom of the barrel, so certain that meditation could help turn their lives around. As Director of the Trust, I never felt we had to "sell" meditation. It certainly was vitally important to me after I entered the convent. There I was taught the value of prayer, and today that insight is ubiquitous. In the last 25 years, there seems to be an invisible net attracting those people who know with great certainty that meditation is therapeutic. It was not surprising to me that some of these people are within the prison population. I am always struck by the fact that the home of a prisoner and a monk are indicated by the same word: cell.

Dr. Carlson's advice seems to be based on Zen itself: "To a great extent our peace of mind is determined by how well we live in the present moment. Surrender yourself to the fact that pity is a self-defeating emotion; and if enduring, we end up feeling sorry for ourselves." He describes compassion as a heart-felt emotion, a further concession that true virtue comes from within, as he says, "from the heart." Zen says compassion spawns from our inner Sacred Nature.

As the story in the previous chapter shows, the Theravadan monk felt that he illustrated the Sacred Power by levitating a chair and himself to the ceiling. Harada Roshi used the same Power for a compassionate service . . . offering a cup of tea to a weary traveller. Which is appropriate? "Selling water by the river" means that Zen deals with very ordinary, everyday stuff; because it is made available by the Sacred Power, it is holy. Zen prefers to say that since every particle of creation is filled with the Sacred, and every action is done by means of the Sacred Power, then everything is Sacred. So what is special about it? It is as common as water.

There might be a tie-in between the above and the mistaken idea some people have about Zen, that it is practiced by noticing our thoughts as they pass. I had a cousin who got her degree in nursing with a thesis entitled *Zen and the Art of Nursing*, which was built on the premise that Zen is watching your passing thoughts. Never mind . . . she got an A! But let's not let the idea pass by too quickly. Imagine a sex offender in prison watching his or her thoughts. No chance of hope and healing there.

When I review the prisoners I have dealt with over the years, I know some that were too wounded for rehabilitation. There is David, whose alcoholic father beat his depressive mother until she committed suicide when he was 2 years old. He was roaming the streets at the age of 4, and taken into a home shortly after. He had been in eight different homes until he was 12, when he ran away, joined a gang, and was arrested for armed robbery by the time he reached 14.

What he needed then was counselling, and accommodation that was user-friendly, the company of young lads his age, understanding adults, sports to work off excess frustration and contact with a religious figure to help him develop spiritually.

What actually transpired was that David was thrown into a cell with an assortment of adult criminals, whose example he emulated by returning kick for kick. Of course eventually he was put in a Young Offenders Institute, but by then he had only one reaction to authority from birth, which was reinforced endlessly by his life situation. In and out of prison many times, he was moved from one to another to give the guards a break from his insolent behavior. It wasn't until his 24th birthday that he decided he did not want to spend the rest of his life in prison. He wrote me that he would like to learn meditation so that he could really "get his head straight" and change.

I decided to go see him on Christmas Day, as much for myself as for him. To visit a prisoner on Christmas Day is a special privilege, for a variety of reasons. One of the Trust's patrons made the arrangements. When I arrived at the prison, I knew things weren't going well. I asked the officer what was wrong, and he replied that David had been allowed out of solitary confinement for the day, and had offered to help in the kitchen. He had an argument with another inmate, on whom he threw a bucket of boiling water, resulting in a 70 percent body burn.

I had taken several hours to get to the prison, but naturally I volunteered immediately to return home. Since I had been cleared by the prison's highest authority as well as its security department, I was taken to a room where I had a long wait. Eventually, David arrived holding up his pants and slopping along in shoes without laces. He explained that he would soon be seeing the police from the local town and any string or belt on his person had been removed in case he attempted suicide.

While writing this book, I regularly look at this particular part of the story, and ask what effect it has had on me and how it may have helped me to become the person I am now. I feel certain that few of us have ever spent Christmas day visiting someone in his 20s in prison. It was quite traumatic, and we were constantly interrupted by prison officers as well as the police. The poor young fellow sat there, scared to death, but it didn't stop him acting tough. "Why, David? Why did you do it?" I asked. "He was buggin' me!"

My heart was pleading for him to be reasonable. He was young enough to be my son, yes, even my grandson, and he was alone on Christmas Day with no one caring for him. Now, nine years and many prisons later, we are still in touch. When people ask me how many hardened prisoners I have met, I can still truthfully reply, I've never met one. Months, years, visits, letters and phone calls later, I persuaded David finally to go to the therapeutic prison which was then under the care of Tim Newell, our Trust's compassionate Trustee. There was change in and for David. For the first time in his many years in prison, he was treated as a person, proudly chose the wall colors for his cell, etc. He called the guards and officers by their first names. When I commented on this, he replied that they called him David, too, which was another first for him in prison.

At the end of my initial visits there was a minor incident. David had risen and turned quickly around to take his jacket from the back of the chair, and I had just started toward him to give a hug. I inadvertently touched him. His automatic reaction was to swing around and give out a swat that would have knocked me over if it had made contact. Fortunately he missed. The guard on duty gave me a frown, and David was appalled when he saw what he had almost done. I tried to placate him, settling instead for a handshake. No ploughshares showing! About eight months later, he invited me to a farewell supper the 36 men on the wing had prepared, and at the end, as I went to shake hands with him for the final goodbye in that prison, he refused the handshake and stepped back, threw open his arms and gave me a wonderful bear-hug. Were the swords finally disappearing? Would ploughshares be possible?

Oh, that I could conclude with a final, happy amen. As I write, I've just received another letter. He is back inside, preparing for trial for the attempted murder of a taxi driver. I expect to see him when I return to England, but I'll probably still be dealing with a sword-carrying David, though I hope somewhat tempered. Some of the psychologists in the therapeutic prison said that David was too damaged to become a self-sufficient person. He has long periods of normality, but unless his life is without too much stress, he would be pushed over the edge.

Getting into the problem of whether or not prisons work is to open a can of worms. It is my experience that in large measure prisons do not work. As the above story relates, poverty is an underlying cause of so much criminal behavior, as are addiction, broken homes, mental illness and lack of parenting skills. I believe that if David had had more help and had recourse to a counselor on a regular basis in the community, he would not have been driven to commit his last offence. Easily the vast majority of the thousands of men and women I have visited or otherwise had contact with in prison need help and psychological treatment.

I can relate stories of ex-prisoners who are not only leading upright and compassionate lives now, but are also devoting their time and skills to helping street kids and the homeless. I can also write about those who will never be released, because they are a continuous threat to themselves and society. They are probably doomed to spend the rest of their lives in a secure hospital. But they are the minority among the prison population, only 30 percent of whom are incarcerated for violent action. What is being done for the majority? The Director of the International Centre for Prison Studies in London, Dr. Andrew Coyle, tells us we get the prisons we deserve. So the onus is on us.

One of the most hopeful experiments in today's field of criminal justice is restorative justice. Its interest extends not only to the offender, but also to the victim and to the local community. To my knowledge it is of Quaker origin, and is described as a new paradigm, based, as far as possible, on repairing the harm caused by crime. It sees the problems with traditional justice, where victims are ignored or even re-victimized by the system. Sentences to denounce crime do not rehabilitate offenders, and rehabilitation does not denounce the seriousness of the offence. Sometimes the emphasis on outcome disregards some harmful effects of the criminal process: for example, the cross-examination of the victim. Traditional justice is based on punishment, which inflicts further harm, stigma, rejection, and unwanted side effects; it makes the offender think of self, not others. Coercion is often used as a first resort. It seems to confuse the issue whereby the court-imposed deterrence is the primary method of crime prevention.

Throughout my time with the Prison Phoenix Trust in Oxford, we tried to live close to the practice of restorative justice. We were in the jurisdiction of the Thames Valley Police, who used the techniques of restorative justice when dealing with young offenders. The officers there spoke with pride about bringing together the offenders and their victims so that they could communicate if they so wished. This involves the victim in the process of reparation while the offender is held accountable. It also enables offenders to earn integration and reacceptance into the community based on consent, where this is possible. Coercion is a last resort. Restorative justice involves the whole community and provides important feedback to its crime prevention agencies. The mediation can be introduced by an adaptation of traditional Western approaches to justice and could be provided countrywide by an independent organization, with supervision by a national body to ensure good standards. Certainly, restorative justice is rapidly becoming a priority in Canada when dealing with young offenders, despite the often rancorous politics that get played out over the Young Offenders Act.

Rather than automatic custody, the offender is given a court referral and a mediation or group conference is organized for those who want to communicate or meet. There is a process of reparation to the victim if desired, and also to the community. Aid and support by the community to both the victim and offender is required. This enables the offender to earn reacceptance by making amends. The system also provides for any victim whose own offender is not caught, as well as for those offenders whose victim is unwilling to take part.

When tough-talking people ask for figures to back up my gospel of transformation for the offender and victim and community, there is evidence in the form of current research that indicates a high success rate. The British town of Leeds is one area where the principles of restorative justice have been developed when working with young offenders. When I was in England, I was shown the figures for Leeds area, where just under half the cases were referred to mediation. Practically all of the offenders (90 percent) said they preferred the process of restorative justice, although some of them were not able to participate in a direct mediation. In another phase in that same area, all of the offenders (fully 100 percent) who did have direct mediation were satisfied, while slightly fewer (93 percent) offenders said it was important to them to be able to tell the victim what happened. Another 62 percent said it was important to negotiate restitution, and 90 percent said it was important to apologize to the victim. In actuality almost all of that 90 percent did apologize.

Restorative justice is more compatible with rehabilitation than punishment. One way of making reparation is to participate in some form of "rehab" program. But this is a two-way requirement. The community *has* to provide education, training, therapy, and above all, employment. As for the victims of these crimes, 80 percent said it was important for them to receive explanations from their offenders about what happened, while 90 percent said it was important for them to tell the offender the impact the crime had on them. Another 73 percent said they wanted an apology, while 65 percent said it was important to negotiate restitution. In an American study, just over one-third of the cases went to mediation. Of these, 95 percent involved negotiated agreements, 58 percent involved financial restitution, while 13 percent resulted in personal service, and another 29 percent in community service. Practically all of the victims (90 percent) and the offenders (91 percent) were satisfied by the outcome. After their experience of mediation, only 18 percent re-offended, while the record shows that 27 percent of those whose cases did not involve mediation re-offended.

What about the majority of our prisoners here in Canada? What can be done here? A recent edition of *Maclean's* magazine (25/12/2000) points out that that 75 percent of Canadians apparently feel that all young offenders, regardless of age, who are accused of violent crimes should be tried in adult courts. Another poll showed that slightly more than half of the respondents (52 percent) thought the death penalty should be re-invoked for first degree murder, while a third (34 percent) think that prison should be used only as a punishment of last resort. It seems that there is no other issue which tests the defining Canadian characteristic of compassion and tolerance as sorely as crime.

The decision of Canada's Supreme Court, handed down early in 2001, condemned the death penalty as an irrevocable horror and unanimously prevented the extradition to the United States of accused Canadians if they faced execution there. The Court said that a recent roll call of wrongful murder convictions both in Canada and the United States provides tragic testimony of the fallibility of our legal systems, despite their elaborate safeguards for the protection of the innocent. Their landmark 9–0 decision says, in part:

> It is final. It is irreversible. Its imposition has been described as arbitrary. Its deterrent value has been doubted. Its implementation necessarily causes psychological and physical suffering. The instances in Canada are few, but if capital punishment had been carried out, the result could have been the killing by the government of innocent individuals.

As a Canadian, I found myself walking a little taller the day of that announcement. Dostoevsky points out in his novel *The Brothers Karamazov* that the tragedy is in what we do to *ourselves* when we commit a crime.

There are obviously some prisoners who will never become well. They will probably always have to be in a secure hospital. For other diseases such as sex offending, we should remember that they are on a scale, too. Some are highly diseased and others less so, and all have varying shades of intensity. Some can be helped. Some cannot. The Law Courts and Prison Officials have unenviable decisions to make.

Last Christmas, I received a present from a woman prisoner who had recently delivered a baby. According to prison regulations, she had to give the child up when she returned to her cell. She went through a whole series of frustrations, and somehow, each one ended with the sound of a child's rattle. Finally she made a rattle herself, using two halves of dried orange skins, some seeds within, the handle made from a broken twig snatched during her daily exercise period out of doors, all secured together with common string. It was the most provocative gift I had received in years.

Although it is never enough, the homeless are receiving considerable attention currently, and just after the last Christmas season, a study was done in London. Most vagrants (70 percent) stated unequivocally they did not want a job, they did not want affordable housing, they did not want to join Alcoholics or Drugs Anonymous. They wanted to stay as they are for the time being, although they admitted that the time might come when they want to change. Then they will ask for help, and not before. The inner longing has not taken hold yet. Some would say they haven't hit rock bottom yet.

Meditation classes sometimes start on the streets of a big city. Sometime in 1980, during the worst of the Marcos years, I was living with the Good Shepherd sisters on Aurora Boulevard in the Quezon City area of Manila (at that time with a population of about 12 million people). One evening I was enjoying our recreation period with the sisters. Over a period of about 10 minutes, one after the other, three or four sisters were called to the phone, and all returned with the same message: "I've just been told that the convent is cordoned off by the military." We knew the phones were tapped, so we could not call outside. In a few minutes, I was summoned to the phone. The caller was a *zendo* member asking if I knew Boy Morales. I heard the inner warning bells ringing and refused to discuss the matter then and there, since the man in question had been a Marcos appointment and later defected to the hills with the New People's Army, which was the only organized opposition to the rapacious dictator.

The next day I met that caller in a nearby restaurant, and she relayed a request from Boy Morales, that I go to his detention center Bago Bantay to teach Zen. He and about 10 other political prisoners who had been tortured needed meditation. Of course I agreed, but knew that I needed to get organized first. I decided to go to the Canadian Embassy for advice. There I found the ambassador, who saw me almost at once. He was quite startled when I asked if he knew Boy Morales and warned that I would be deported within a week if I went to the prison. I told him the question wasn't "if" but rather "how," and so the ambassador excused himself, went to another room and returned about 10 minutes later with his first councillor. "We've decided to tell you that we know Boy Morales very well and have helped him several times in his work in rural areas," they began, and to my relief I knew I might find allies here.

The outcome was that General Verr, the Marcos regime's henchman and head of the military and Intelligence, had recently visited the embassy in order to get some information about Canadian universities for a family member. The ambassador was able to help him. The day of my visit, he picked up the phone and got through immediately to Verr and asked for a return favor, that I be able to go to Bago Bantay to help Boy Morales and, at the same time, be assured of complete safety. General Verr agreed. And thus it happened. Eventually, Morales was to say that my concurrence with the embassy had saved his life. The Intelligence knew I was in contact with the embassy, and they also knew that I visited Boy regularly each Friday. So they could not make him disappear as so many other prisoners had.

Torture with electric nodes, a method used on the Bago Bantay detainees, leaves the victim jumpy and nervy. There were other ways of torture, too, more primitive, but nevertheless effective. One man said his head was held under water until a second or two before he would pass out. This was repeated several times in succession. There were revelations, too, about the pain endured when a carbonated drink was sprayed on the sensitive tissue inside the nose and throat.

On my first visit, I saw only Morales. Quite often and regularly, he would shake and shiver violently. He said he would like me to give the Orientation talks to the group (there were eight or ten internees). They would come to my weekly class together, and sit together each day at noon when the firing range next door was silent. I gave a resume of the talks to the first gathering, which the camp director attended. We all had a set of cushions, and I can clearly remember that ragamuffin group of detainees sitting with the smartly uniformed officer, as they all listened and then started *zazen*.

Morales's scheme worked. Every Friday at 10 a.m., I was allowed to bring a casserole of vegetables with me, which we ate at noon, accompanying the rice cooked by the one detainee who would not sit. The prisoners sit twice a day, an hour at noon and on their bunks each evening, Morales himself doing two, three or even four hours. It was no surprise at all that three or four of them eventually came to *kensho.*

During those days, there was tension throughout the country. In many ways it was worse in the countryside. The military held the people in terror and quite often someone would disappear and never be seen again. I remember riding my Honda 50 around the barrios in southern Leyte, helping farmers with their pig problems, in the sights of the military all the time. They would have discovered from the locals that I was not proselytizing against Marcos as some foreign missioners were. The NPA soldiers did not hinder me, although they checked on my work constantly to see that it really was in the best interests of the poor. I joined my OLM sisters, with whom I was living, in attending one of the many courses Church groups (branded "radical," of course) ran, as we tried to understand what was wrong with the system.

The talks were heavy on Marx, and naturally the basis of the problem was the structure of Philippine society and government. One thing I'll never forget. For a weekend, everyone would arrive in sneakers (which means they were not poor) and immediately change to *chinellas,* to show their solidarity with the poor, who wore hardly anything else. They certainly all knew the lingo.

Oddly enough, I often felt in familiar territory during those meetings, perhaps because of the talks Larry and I had had on social justice. He had never lived in an oppressive country, but his Jesuit training had taught him of the north and south economic polarities along with other issues involving the works of social justice, which became *his* issues. I also recall first hearing the word "dysfunctional" during one of our musical breaks. I began to reflect on my own closeted existence, which extended from entering religious life in 1953, through 12 years in the Kansai area of Japan where English newspapers were few, until 1973 when I went to Kamakura and started to have doors opened for me. I soon realized how cut off I had been from so much of the outside world. In many ways, I resembled Rip Van Winkle. In regard to social justice issues, apart from the balance Larry tried to demonstrate, I was left quite ignorant. Once I got to the Philippines in 1976, though, the indignities heaped upon the population by the Marcos regime provided me with a quick and decisive leap in the direction of compassion. Despite the frenzy of the social justice pull, my regular Zen meditation kept me focused and free. There were seminars on all sides as we studied not personalities but structures. The leader in opposition to the government then was the NPA, the euphemistic hope for democracy. Some church people went overboard in their enthusiastic support for the rebels, and I visited convents where ammunition supplies were housed en route to the hills. There were avaricious brutalities and ambitious pride on both sides.

After Ninoy Aquino was assassinated in 1985, the ambiguity cleared a bit, as the middle class awoke and acknowledged what was obvious to an increasing number of us. A third force mobilized, spearheaded in Manila, and we were off and running. The first big demonstration was organized in Manila, and the Good Shepherd Sisters, at whose convent I was staying, were asked to participate. We assembled with two or three hundred teachers and others on the Jesuit Ateneo campus and were sternly lectured that there might be violence. We were expected to protect the workers and the poor with whom we would meet up when we arrived in the center of the city. We were to take the brunt of the brutality. We were divided into groups of 20, enclosed within a yellow roped circle. Each group contained one doctor or nurse and one lawyer in case we were injured or arrested. We were then asked to kneel as we received absolution.

It all sounds dramatic now, compared to the sophisticated way demonstrations eventually got organized. That day we marched down to Santa Cruz Church, where we were given 30 minutes to relax. I stepped aside to allow a man to leave the church, and I couldn't believe my eyes. It was the police officer who had accosted me at Muntinlupa prison the week before, suspecting me of working with the underground. Anyway, this day he was coming out of the church wearing a yellow T-shirt which read I LOVE NINOY. It was my best laugh of the day!

Although it is rather naïve, I considered working with both sides on the spiritual level. There were so many sad events in the countryside. Young people feel so deeply, and there was considerable rabble rousing. One incident remains engraved in my heart. It happened when I was down in Hinunangan, Leyte. One night, at about 12:50 a.m., there was a gunshot in front of the convent, our small, four-bedroom wooden home. We were right across the street from the Municipio, the local government center, and the police station where the military were holed up. That started an entire night of terror. Shots and explosives and fire bombs rained from dark to dusk. The New People's Army had descended from the hills. For all of two minutes, perhaps, I lay in bed, thinking. Then a sister who had just arrived crawled into my room and asked what was happening. So we got up and at first decided to lie on the floor to miss the stray bullets. We recited the rosary together. Then we discovered the need to communicate. It was the night of November 30, St. Andrew's Day 1979, and some of us had Scottish blood in our veins. In any case, we couldn't resist peeking out of the windows. I recall there was no moon, no electricity of course, so it was very dark, and we could see nothing but the fire bombs as they went off. I remember thinking I would like to do *zazen* and keep the inner racket at bay, but for the sake of the other sisters who did not pray that way, I held on to the rosary and made small, which was really big, talk. As dawn approached the firing stopped abruptly and the invaders returned to the mountains. The townspeople who had relatives and friends in the military surged out of their houses with thermoses of hot coffee for the weary soldiers. It had been a long night.

So I was alert but not particularly worried a year later in Manila, when the phone call to teach prisoners came. I had experience enough to put off the caller doing business over the phone but did agree to meet her the next day at a public restaurant. As far as I could tell, I was not followed leaving the convent, nor as I entered the restaurant. It was months later that I learned of the sophisticated means the Intelligence, under General Verr, had at their disposal. His men may already have been waiting for us to meet and recorded every word we said. Someday, I may get a chance to read those military reports. I spent about four years going to Bago Bantay Detention Centre each Friday. Concerned friends drove me at first, but when I discovered their car licence was recorded, I travelled the last several blocks on foot, zigzagging the route. What I experienced inside the prison convinced me to spend the rest of my life accompanying incarcerated people to healing and spiritual fulfillment through meditation.

It is when teaching in prisons that I realize anew the great value a proper body position supports when sitting. The political prisoners at Bago Bantay were especially keen and disciplined. The mental flow activity to silence was also practiced diligently. I never felt we meditation teachers got this same smooth adjustment in prisons for criminals, where the atmosphere is especially hostile. Even while sitting, it is a long time before inmates are able to lower their line of vision and feel secure.

To those readers who may start to sit while reading this book, I would like to say a little more about Zen. In the previous chapter we returned to the cushions, seeing our meditation as an extension of the work we have just left and to which we will be returning. The essential underlying unity has its counterpart in our practice, in the aspect of a constant openness. We became aware of the fact that we do not sit alone but as one who has embraced all of life, the whole family of creation, from a minute microorganism to the most advanced human being. We mentioned the effects of the power that is generated in that absorption process.

A further word and another caution of a probable irritant during sitting. Beginners very soon get crowded off the cushion by what we call linear thinking. It often develops into a complete scenario, with people and comments appearing and disappearing on the screen of the mind. When we become aware of this serial, we put it gently aside, and return to counting our breath. Generally speaking, linear thinking seems to bother beginners more than seasoned sitters. When you catch yourself, return "home" and be firm in determining not to visit the past or future while sitting. The *zafu* is for *zazen* and the present moment only.

After deepening to a certain extent, the bouts of linear thinking become fewer. However, we are often bothered by a solitary mental projection, a random thought. At such a time, we have probably lost the breath-count and an idea pops up on the screen of the mind. We soon become aware of the intruder and, after acknowledging its presence, put it aside gently and resume breath-counting.

There is something more or less natural about random thoughts. Yamada Roshi used to refer to them as the wisps of cloud that pass before Mount Fuji. They come for a moment, and then pass away. Try not to let them mean more to you than that. Sleepiness and staleness are two conditions we have to contend with at times. Splashing cold water on the face or doing a few bending exercises at the end of *kinhin* (walking meditation) are extremely helpful. Or in a *zendo*, perhaps a couple of well-placed contacts with the *kyosaku* (the stick to smooth out an aching shoulder) will help! With perseverance, success is possible. Indeed, when sitting well, the process takes over, and we are no longer aware of our thoughts or even our aching knees. We just ARE.

In my prison experience, I found that by sitting and trying to practice Zen spirituality, the *sangha* gradually changed their swords into ploughshares. It soon became noticeable to me that their bodies responded to the discipline and became less agitated, and finally silent. As a social group, the prisoners had been sullen, argumentative and enervated under the watchful eye of trainees from the Intelligence department, where Bago Bantay was situated. But gradually they started to change from an angry, tense and incapacitated group to a relaxed, sociable, energized and effective team.

After his *kensho* experience, one prisoner was to write me:

> I am perfectly free, I am perfectly happy, and deeply at peace. This was possible, because even though in prison, I have tasted that true ONENESS you led me to in meditation. That night back in my cell I slept soundly like a baby, with a smile on my lips. Now I know that where I am and where I want to be are no different at all! The bars and stone walls do not really separate me from my loved ones, from my friends, from my people, and from everything and everybody in the universe. In reality, I and the universe are one. Thank you.

Chapter Nine

Within the Esoteric

Some years ago, I found myself wanting to paraphrase the statement of the popular East–West guru Bede Griffiths, in that I, too, could perceive a golden thread weaving royal patterns in my life story. But as I reflect on it all from the standpoint of *biju* (the word for one's 77th birthday year, meaning filled with joy and happiness), I find the gold is charged. The thread is not only of precious substance, but also a continuous conductor of life and energy and power.

A monk introduced himself to the teacher Hsuan-sha (Gensha Shibi), saying, "I have just entered this monastery. Please show me where to enter the Way."

"Do you hear the sound of the valley stream?" asked Hsuan-sha.

"Yes," said the monk.

"Enter there."

Zen teaches us that the essence of the sound of the valley stream *can* be perceived. Its sound is strident. The stridency is yet another link between meditation and music. It happens when we put resin on the hair of the violin bow. Under a microscope, a resined bow hair looks like a saw with many teeth. At present, most violinists use aluminium wound strings, and therefore a well-resined bow is a necessity, not only to maintain the adherence of the bow to the smooth string surface, but also to produce this strident quality. All good string players cultivate it. It is not necessarily a tone of loud timbre, although I often wonder if some rock musicians try to emulate that strident quality by sheer volume. That day in 1946 at the Juilliard ensemble class, Arthur Winograd played every note of that Brahms melody in beautiful but strident tone. Judy Garland had it in her voice, as does Barbra Streisand. An orchestra produces it *en masse*. When present, the stridency shoots the message straight to the heart. I recall coming across a musician reduced to tears as she played and replayed a recording of a well-known soprano singing *The Swan* by Grieg. Its intensity held her captive.

I recall a conversation with Fr. Enomiya-Lassalle (himself a cellist) concerning this. He claimed that although it seemed to come primarily from the bow, there had to be an equal pressure by the left-hand fingertips on the strings. For him, this was what string playing was all about. Of course, too much of it and we cry with sore ear drums. But if there is none, the music slips through ineffectively. Singers either have it or don't have it. I recognized this quality at an early age. When I was young, we had a screened-in porch upstairs where I was allowed to sleep during the summer months. One night Louis Armstrong and his band played in a hall across the street. That was the first time I remember perceiving this quality in myself. The last time was when I heard Stephen Isserlis play the slow Adagio movement of the Brahms 2nd Sonata for cello and piano. If I had to illustrate that strident quality I would play his recording of that work. Of course he also had the Feuhermann

Stradivarius cello on loan from Japan. A sensitive instrument helps.

What has this to do with meditation? There are various ways for a disciple to sit in Zen meditation, in breath counting, *shikantaza*, and/or using the *koan* Joshu's Dog. In the first two instances, sitters gradually sink into silence, and the breath forms the link between body and *kokoro* (heart-mind). Gradually, when all things are ready, they forget the self and the Great Matter presents Itself in a small or maybe deep experience. In the third instance, the practice is slightly different, at least in the early stages, and an abrasive sound is given. The teacher must monitor this closely, but it causes the sitter to move along more quickly to experience. I have often wondered about this abrasive strident quality, and I certainly do not assign it to every sitter who comes to me. However, it *does* work. It brings us to the sound of the valley stream.

We know what meditation is supposed to effect, but what about music? What is music supposed to effect? The philosopher Jacques Maritain has written that a great composition in the minor key moves us right to the throne of God. Of course it is presupposed we are capable of being moved. He also says there is an incompleteness in the minor key that urges us on to completeness. In other words, it moves us. That is when and what music effects. Unfortunately, it can move us to unseemly places. It can be the same for silence. Sometimes in a meditation circle in prison we spot a fantasizer: the chin comes up, there is a silly smile on the lips, and the body sways ever so slightly. The sitter is in an unhealthy place. I go right to that person to redirect him or her.

But most often we see a face that changes, eyes stay partially closed, mouth lines soften, cheeks relax, and a soft featuring suffuses the entire face. I know that the sitter is approaching the sacred, the home of the esoteric. There is no worry for the teacher. We are moved to the esoteric when we sit if there are no detaining blocks or ego impulses. Music isn't the only art of transport. When I look at some of Lawren Harris's Arctic scenes in Larisey's book, *Light for a Cold Country*, I am moved. They are stark and strident and moving.

There is a fascination concerning the mystery of the esoteric. It is said the esoteric is for the initiated disciples of a true teacher. If we take "disciple" to mean discipline, then we are dealing with what I call the authentic esoteric. For me it is identifiable with the sacred. And sacred is more than just an adjective. As a noun, IT is in upper case. As an adjective, it is less demanding and sometimes, unfortunately, acquiesces to the demands of those who identify IT only as energy. The esoteric is the meeting place of the human and the sacred, and in His goodness, God has generously gifted the Orient. I cannot describe it, but IT has become my only destiny just as IT has fascinated millions of others.

It certainly captured the mind and heart of one of the most attractive and puzzling mystics in the last century, the Trappist monk and prolific author Thomas Merton. His autobiography, *The Seven Storey Mountain*, took the world and myself by storm in the late 1940s. He continues to inspire, though some of his adventures and stories confuse, too. His ubiquitous sightings of the sacred, found in his later works, try the patience of some of his closest friends, and yet he continued to spell out precisely how his spirituality was working itself out in his daily life as a monk and hermit. More theses and books about him are produced every year, and they often tell us more about the writer than the subject. I read somewhere that Merton himself felt that biographies of the Virgin Mary *are* in fact autobiographies of the authors.

When Merton's writings about Zen came into my hands, I was amazed. He seemed to have had an intuitive grasp of

Zen. Daisetsu Suzuki, with whom he met, is not a heavy-weight, according to contemporary Japanese Zen Masters. Many feel Suzuki did not experience a deep *satori*. His temple life was short, but his role in history was crucial since he opened the door to Oriental meditation for Westerners and whetted their appetite for Zen. Merton was one of his advocates.

It is difficult to say whether Merton knew of Suzuki's Zen caliber. Maybe he felt he had just met another famous writer of Zen spirituality with whom he could connect at that level. I was offered the opportunity to go to the Merton Center at Bellarmine University in Louisville, Kentucky, and have access to all of Merton's writings and underline anything I felt had evolved from an experience. Alas, this invitation came at an inopportune time for me, and I declined.

I continued to read Merton and think that his hunger for God and intimacy are well served in his writings. He certainly felt the Oriental wisdom was of God. The progress he made in prayer is well along Zen lines. There is a stridency in its spirituality, which brings forth a strong approach to art. A true contemplative, living within this kind of energy potential, cannot do nothing. One is compelled to action. And in ratio with the authenticity of the doer, the action will be appropriate. Merton soon took to silence alone and courageously, moving from his cell in the Abbey of Gethsemani to a hermitage in the abbey grounds. He pressed forth where IT bid him go forth. He was seemingly catapulted out of his cell and, through his books, into the international marketplace of ideas. That is what contemplation does. It gets you involved in the world's problems. Merton's concerns were all over the world. He certainly touched something of that inner core, that esoteric center of contemplation. Rather than divert his attention away from the world, this fuelled him with a seeming oversupply of impetus to do something about the many social concerns that he took on.

Zen considers IT as the inner source of all appropriate actions. IT can only be en-fired from within. And of course it must be disciplined. One *has* to be courageous, because one is proceeding from inner urgings, not according to plans set up by the government or its agencies. With the hindsight history gives us, we can see that although Merton's actions seemed controversial at the time, now they are seen as appropriate. There are even indications that the FBI–CIA were concerned with his insights. If that is so, it was a little ridiculous for them to think they could stifle or redirect that flow, if indeed they really tried.

They *did* try with me. When I was in the Philippines during the worst of the Marcos era, a lot of Filipino dissidents came to the *zendo*. One of our members had a friend in the American Embassy, and heard that "they" were going to send someone to investigate just what I was doing. I met with the members of the *zendo* committee who helped me with Filipino issues. They agreed with my gut feeling, that we should let that person join and go through orientation like anyone else. And this we did. I don't know what he – let's call him "Robert"– made of the *teisho* and *dokusan*, but eventually he balked on the *koans*. He wanted to know the inside story and in fact demanded it. I retorted that he would have to discover for himself, just like everyone else, through experience.

He had the choice of the door, or a long gruelling practice and, to give him credit, he chose the latter, even following me to Singapore, where I travelled twice a year for *sesshin*. The acting head of the group there was an American whose father had been in the navy. One look at our Robert and he phoned a warning to me immediately. "That guy has CIA written all over him, name, haircut and all. Do you realize this?" Robert, of course, stayed in a nearby hotel, and came late in the mornings so that he could get in his daily run. This would never have been countenanced in Kamakura, but I relented, and Robert and I both persevered. He came to experience, and eventually retired from the Marines, becoming interested in the kind of prison work I was doing in England, and started his own initiative at home. In the end we were both winners.

I cannot articulate what grasp of the esoteric Robert holds, but when I first met him, he exemplified the fear, ignorance and nervousness the military has of the spiritual. At that time, I was also under surveillance by the Philippine military. One of our members was picked up and questioned for 12 hours by several prominent officials and intelligence officers. They asked her to account for her weekly visit to the Good Shepherd Chapel and they accused her, and us, of sitting on the floor. She was asked: What real Christian group would ever sit on the floor? The generals said they had never seen real nuns and real priests sit on the floor to meditate and *never* facing the wall!

The Orient has a history of going to mystics in times of doubt, or disaster, or drought, and seeking wisdom. In the West, we send in the Intelligence agency. On a regular basis, the officers at Bago Bantay Detention Centre would take me into an office with the reminder that they knew why I was really there, and that I was carrying information from the underground. As a showdown (and the eventual revolution) was obviously approaching, I became bolder and assured them I knew that they were quite aware of what the meditation was effecting in the lives of the detainees. I would certainly love to read their internal reports one day.

One can, of course, be deceived into thinking the esoteric has been achieved and inner lights are authentic and appropriate. That is why a legitimate teacher is necessary. Alone and on one's own, one can easily be deceived. I reiterate Dogen's caution: "One should not do *zazen* without a teacher." In the deeper state of consciousness, all can be trusted. It is not necessarily so with objective meditation.

179

I am often asked about the contrast of silent prayer and what I call soul prayer – prayer with an object. Here we are in the realm of Christian prayer, and it is not without its gift, too. That great woman Teresa of Avila had many visions. They were for her alone and were very helpful. She could speak of the love that God has for us with warmth and conviction. John of the Cross is said, though, to have given her friendly warning that she was seeing too much. Many mystics of her day had voluble conversations with the Lord, and were gifted with visions. We do hear of isolated cases where the visions are authentic, but generally they are outnumbered by the spurious.

Do people in Zen have visions? Yes, they do, but they are not considered vital to the practice. At a deep state of consciousness, one does not perceive any objectivity. As I have said innumerable times, there is no-thing in the Essential world. If there is an object, then one is not in the appropriate place. These misperceptions are called *makyo*. Before I deal with this subject, I'd like to clear up another misconception: that Zen sitters are beaten into *kensho* with a stick. This stick, called a *kyosaku,* lies on the altar of each *zendo* throughout the world.

A *kyosaku* is literally for encouragement. It is about three feet long, flattened to a width of 8 cm at one end, and rounded at the other to provide easy handling. It is usually used during *sesshin,* and only with permission of the *zendo's* highest authority. It is treated with deep respect and compassion. We say that it is a service we teachers render, to reactivate the clusters of blood vessels found at the base of the neck. The *kyosaku* is also a strident instrument.

It is very often misunderstood in pseudo-Zen circles, where gory stories of its use abound. Unfortunately, with the present dearth of legitimate Zen teachers in Japan today, the custodians of the many beautiful *zendos* throughout the Japanese countryside find that their maintenance bills can be paid by generously using this stick on curious tourists who want a taste of Zen.

The use of the *kyosaku* (also called the *keisaku* "correction stick" in other Zen traditions) began in China and was intended then to gently arouse a sleepy sitter. A branch of a tree was used, and the rustling sound of dried leaves at the ear of a drowsy sitter was enough to ensure a return to waking consciousness. Over the years, the bough was replaced by a stick, which came to be used as a stimulant for the cluster of blood vessels under the muscles at either side of the base of the neck. Anyone who has had a vigorous *shiatsu* (massage) rubdown will appreciate how a well-administered clout can feel.

Adachi Roshi, so often our monitor in Kamakura, says that he uses the *kyosaku* now almost exclusively in response to a request. Some sitters find it extremely helpful. Others do not. The extent to which it is used is up to the sitters generally. If we feel the need, we perform a *gassho* (palms of hands together) when we are aware that the monitor is making the rounds with the stick.

With the help of the *kyosaku*, *sangha* members and a teacher, our sitting gradually deepens. A delicate refinement and harmony of body and spirit, mind and breath develops and affects us in many beautiful ways. Our long-held biases and blocks start to loosen their grip, and we feel a little of the freedom that is our birthright. The most unpromising people do change. The delicate journey to sitting in perfect oneness is a long, slow path, and until inner freedom is attained to some degree there may be certain maladjustments of body and spirit, mind and breath that produce sensations, which of course must be dealt with.

In our concentration, thought waves on the surface of the consciousness are partially calmed, and elements of past experience in the subconscious are liable to surface. These are called *makyo* (literally "external devils"). Depending on the individual, they may be either pleasant or unpleasant, but never good or bad. *Makyo* is always neutral and must be resolutely set aside. It should be reported to the teacher, however, for it gives some indication of how the sitter is progressing.

Makyo is usually a visual or aural representation. It used to be more prevalent in the early, noisy days of Zen practice. When Yasutani Roshi was still alive, his way more or less prevailed. The four monitors would brandish their *kyosaku* as they hollered encouragement, and many participants pressed down on their practice quite audibly. There was frequent *makyo*.

With Yamada Roshi and his successors, a quieter Zen prevails. The *Roshi* felt that Shakyamuni's Zen was quiet, as was that of the great teachers Joshu and Dogen. This way fosters a natural ripening, prolonged a bit, perhaps, but leading to a harmonizing experience. Quiet Zen seems to bypass *makyo* to a great extent. Toward the end of his life, Yamada Roshi said that probably only 15 percent of the sitters in his *zendo* experienced *makyo*.

In my own case, while still studying with Fukagai Roshi, I had been asked by Fr. Enomiya-Lassalle to help with the first English *sesshin* at his *zendo* west of Tokyo, called Shinmeikutsu (Cave of Divine Darkness). Being overseer left me a fair amount of time to sit. Within a couple of days, I began to hear a radio. When I complained to the janitor, he assured me there wasn't one in the area. The following day, I noticed the radio played only when I was sitting and not busy in the kitchen or answering the phone.

One afternoon while sitting in the *zendo*, I was drowsy in the heat, and my head must have nodded. In any case, one of the rookie monitors rushed up, and without any indication of his intention, gave me a couple of good solid whacks with the *kyosaku*. Immediately the "radio" burst into loud majestic musical chords, which seemed to come from a heavenly organ. Its sound filled the entire universe, and lasted for several minutes, then gradually grew less in volume, and within an hour or so disappeared completely. I never heard it again.

I recognized the *makyo* and related it to Fr. Lassalle that evening. He advised me to change teachers and train under one whose name was being frequently mentioned in Zen circles, Yamada Koun Roshi. Within a few months, a *kensho* was confirmed during *rohatsu sesshin*, the weeklong, annual winter retreat prior to the anniversary of Shakyamuni's enlightenment.

There is a widely held belief that Christianity considers most visions and their proclamations and miracles as authentic manifestations of God. I would like to point out that the Church has always taught that God *can* intervene and communicate with humans. But the Church is very clear that such manifestations are usually for the individual alone and not necessarily a direct experience of God. The same wise old Church has always discouraged this kind of phenomenon, for we have a good history of persecuting our mystics.

The reason for this reticence is that visions can arise solely from the human psyche, and in our phraseology are wholly *makyo*. There is, of course, a difficult discernment to be made in determining the authenticity of a mystical revelation, and experience has taught that the visual and auditive forms that arise from the ego far outnumber the ones that come from heaven.

St. John of the Cross teaches us to ignore them all. In *Ascent of Mount Carmel* he writes:

> I say then, that with regard to all these visions and apprehensions and to all forms and species whatsoever, which represent themselves beneath some particular kind of knowledge or image or form, whether they be false and come from the devil, or recognized as true and coming from God, we must not feed upon them, nor must the soul desire to receive them, lest it shall no longer be detached, free, pure and simple, as is required for union. The reason for this is that all these forms have limitations and that the Wisdom of God wherewith we are to be united contains no limit because it is wholly pure and simple, and God comes not with any image or form or kind of intelligence.

To arrive at this point "with no form or kind of intelligence" requires power. For our part, this power is generated by the sitting itself. The late Father de Mello used to call it revelation, and the revelation which silence brings is not knowledge. Revelation is power, a mysterious power which in Japanese Zen is named *joriki* (*jo* is "settling" and *riki* is "power").

Joriki is the power of strength which arises when the mind has been silenced and unified and brought to one-pointedness in *zazen* and awareness in daily life. It is a dynamic power that, once mobilized, enables us to act more intuitively. Indeed, the ancient masters teach us that even in the most sudden and unexpected situations we can act instantly and appropriately in a situation without pausing to collect our wits. Under the power and strength of *joriki,* we are no longer totally ruled by passion nor at the mercy of our environment. We thus gain some measure of true freedom and true equanimity. In other words, Zen teaches that *joriki* is the power that transforms our swords into ploughshares.

In steady sitting, this power builds up, and as it deepens there may be short experiences of entering *samadhi* (Sanskrit) or *zammai* (Japanese), a state deeper than normal consciousness.

It is not a common occurrence and usually happens during *sesshin* on the third or fourth day. It is a deep state of absorption wherein the faculties are in abeyance, and only when the sit is over is one aware of the "empty" and quick passage of time. As I said, it usually happens well into the retreat, and each sit of 25 minutes seems to be just a few minutes. It can also last a few hours, and under its influence one can participate in *kinhin* (walking meditation) without surfacing to normal consciousness. It is sometimes described as the time when the practice takes over. This state too should be reported to the *Roshi* during the regular visit to the *dokusan* room (where Zen repartee takes place). It indicates deep sitting.

There are interesting experiments in Japan and the United States with sophisticated machines that monitor what transpires in the human body during *zazen*. Electrodes are attached to different points on the body of the sitter, and the monitoring is indicated on a dial, not unlike an ordinary radio dial. I was told that on the machine I was studying, the area between the numbers 12 and 22 constituted the peace and creativity area of the brain. As we watched, the weak impulse of the alpha waves became stronger the longer the person sat.

I have a friend in California working with a group experimenting in alpha biofeedback. The waves emanating from the brain are picked up and magnified, and then fed back to the sitter. Hearing one's own alpha waves apparently excites the brain to greater activity in that area. Since alpha waves emanate from the peace area of the brain, one experiences peace giving and peace receiving. My friend claims that she and her associates have helped many people with stress problems. As I remember, the members of the group are all psychologists. They are elated and hopeful for even higher goals, such as a *kensho* experience itself. Yamada Roshi's response to all this was rather reserved: "They've not produced *kensho* yet, and they won't! There is no *kensho* without sore knees!"

Everyone who has tasted the good effects of Zen (and even some who have not) readily credit *zazen* for cures of psychosomatic illnesses. This is true. There are, though, certain mental disorders that are heightened by all the inward concentration necessary in Zen. It is generally conceded by Zen masters that good mental health is a prerequisite in Zen.

Practicing Zen is not all one great rising curve. As the *Roshi* used to say, it is sitting *yurusareta joken de* (in the conditions granted), and with no manipulation. There will be ups and downs, but through them all, a steady conviction that this is the Way for me. There are many small (and big) stepping stones that become very noticeable to a teacher. Little virtues and big ones start appearing as the fruit of sitting. Most Zen masters do not pass out bouquets. They should not have to. Sitting brings its own rewards.

All Oriental meditation is simplicity itself. When asked to speak about its characteristics, I usually describe it as

- Non-objective and directed inward
- Breath-centered; its matter is not contained in words, ideas, concepts, feeling or imagination
- Body participation, it involves the whole person
- A long apprenticeship, a legacy to be received/ bequeathed
- A master–disciple relationship, it cannot be learned through books
- Use of *koans*, all things and nothing
- Experience-oriented
- Healing and transforming, a discipline
- Means and end coalesce.

We start with the dictum "Pray as you can and allow yourself to be led." This is underlined by Yamada Roshi's response which has meant so much to me over the years. When I asked him what he thought meditation should be for the Christian, he immediately replied, "It should be the same as for the Buddhist. Meditation is light sitting in light." In Christian terms, it seems to me that something of this is caught in the word Abba (Father).

A mystic's pilgrimage is not a journey to a holy external shrine, but to an inner Sacred place. I have found in my journey that following this method, plus a little courage and Spartan spirit and with the help of grace, we can conquer inner space. Like modern scientists learning the secrets of the moon, we can be led to enter the land of the sun and find the light and warmth we seek so assiduously.

The journey to the esoteric sacred place is helped by individual instruction (*dokusan*) and public instruction (*teisho*). Both have to do with *koans*. They can be on any subject whatsoever. Within this wide range of objects, the *koans* are all pointing to the same Reality, with a lightness that belies their ultimate value. These marvellous creations of the ancient Chinese masters keep teasing the intellect to admit that it has limitations. And when it surrenders with an "Ah!" there is a moment of sheer joy and delight. As a Zen student, I found *koans* to be a most delightful means of learning, and consider them a worthy standard for the spiritual genius of the Orient.

In working on the *koan* Mu, eventually the apparent gap between ourselves and Mu lessens and we suddenly become one with it. In the action of becoming one with something, we break down the illusive barriers that seem to separate us. We soon come to realize that suffering is caused by this illusion, namely separation. There is a way of reading the New Testament writings of Paul to see that there is only one sin, that of separation. In action, we are one with the real situation. The secret is to be or to do and not to think.

Once when I was teaching English at a steel company in Japan, I was asked what I would exclaim if I knocked over something accidentally. I thought for a moment or two and then offered a suggestion. The men were apparently not convinced and later simulated an awkward situation so that I eventually knocked over a glass of water. Extemporaneously I exclaimed something quite different from the considered reply. A spontaneous response is closer to the center. In Zen, second thoughts are not always desirable. A *koan* is not a verbal game. It incites intuition. Not only the content of the *koan*, but the manner of presentation must be vigorous, spontaneous, and "one with." A *koan* is anti-intellectual only in the sense that the intellect cannot bring us to the Zen experience.

In a *zendo*, one frequently hears the Chinese story of the 500 stupid monkeys. Walking along together one night, the first monkey happened to look down a well by the side of the road, and saw the moon. He was disturbed and called his companions to look at it too. They all shared his dismay that the moon might drown in that well, and then there would be no light at night. So they resolved to save the moon. The first monkey lowered his body into the well by entwining his arms around a nearby tree. The second monkey climbed down and entwined his arms through the curved tail of the first monkey, and so down the well they went, forming a ladder to its depths. Just as the 500th monkey was climbing down to be the one to save the moon, the tree broke, and they all drowned in the deep darkness of their delusion.

A *koan* attempts to lead us to direct experience. In our training, we do not sit with *koans* in the sense of trying to figure them out while we are sitting. We sit harmonized in body and mind, with whatever our practice is. We deal with *koans* in *dokusan* and *teisho*. The subject matter of *koans* has to do with ordinary, simple, everyday things, like dogs and fingers and foxes and bears and trees and flowers. Certain religious people express alarm that these subjects are not overtly religious. Obviously for them there is a sacred and a secular. In the great reality there is no separation.

When I glance away from the screen of this word processor, I see a fir tree, which is not Christian, not Buddhist, but just a fir tree. When you read or hear "fir tree," you have your own internal picture of the tree. If there are 100 people reading this text, then 100 fir trees will appear, and they will all be different. If I should use the word "God" in a *teisho* in front of 35 people, I am aware that 35 different gods appear on their minds' screen. These are conceptualized gods. Concepts are fine in theory, but they kill *koans*. A tree is a *koan* par excellence, as has been attested by several of our members. In Zen spirituality, the word "secular" is not a reality.

Koan subjects are very concrete and act merely as a momentary catalyst, and are not intended as material for contemplation or intrinsic debate. The Oriental master would remind us that doing, thinking and feeling objectify the world, and put us in the ambience of separation, where the ego is strengthened. Here I offer a word of caution to spiritual directors who overuse the multiplying methods suggested in Western psychology to strengthen the ego. If there is a psychological problem, then psychotherapy may be indicated, but I have always felt it is a risky business for any healthy person – an Oriental in particular – to be in a process of ego strengthening for an extended period of time. This goes contrary to the basic tenets of Oriental spirituality and their birthright. For an Occidental, there is already a mind–overload, which needs reducing. For them, *zazen* is at first an antidote.

One time, an American priest who professed an ignorance of Zen said Mass at the Zen Center, Philippines, and during the homily blurted out, "I don't know much about Zen, but you know, all *you* can really do in contemplative prayer is mortification." He understood Zen better than he thought, although I would have added the word gratitude. We may not be inclined to call our silencing mortification, but it is. John of the Cross calls it "the dark night of the soul," and David in the Psalms speaks of "the valley of the shadow of death." We do not pretend to understand all of its ramifications, but discipline does bring about a harmony of body and psyche, and the unifying dynamism speaks its own language which we can all appreciate.

One of the signs of decadence in Japanese Zen training centers over the past two centuries is the existence of books of answers to *koans*, which come from an oral transmission. When celibacy died in Japanese Buddhism, Zen teachers married and had families, and the potent custom of *chonan* (eldest son) inheriting the father's station continued to prevail. Even if the son knew nothing about *koan* and *satori*, he had to take over his father's position as *Roshi*. For a small fee or favor from indigent old-timers, the problem was overcome. So in some cases, *koans* were robbed of their vigor and very life.

Yes, a *koan* is abrasive. It is the side of the box that brings the match to light. It provides the rough edge that moves us along. As we proceed with our sitting in Zen, especially in the hothouse of a *sesshin* (Zen retreat), we sometimes experience a few hours of *zammai* (Japanese) or *samadhi* (Sanskrit) passive meditation. After that, we often start "moving," as we say. Not physically in any way, but moving to a deeper state of consciousness, and we realize we are somehow more sensitized and able to respond to the *Roshi's* thrusts in a more direct and appropriate manner. *Dokusan* (interview) becomes a battlefield of sorts, and many opposing factors come to the fore, as teacher and disciple develop a sparring relationship which can end in *kensho*. Because this is often very colorful and helpful, in the

Sanbo Kyodan we are permitted to write about our *kensho* after it has been confirmed. During the evening of December 6, 1972, I participated in such a joust with Yamada Koun Roshi. On December 30, I submitted to him the following document:

This Joy, This Perfect Joy, Is Now Mine

What are the factors that bring one to *kensho*? I am sure they are different for everyone. The following is a collection of thoughts which seems to have been relevant in bringing about an experience which culminated on December 6, 1972, in Kamakura, Japan.

I was born near the Atlantic Ocean in eastern Canada, into a family where art in many of its forms abounded. As children, we were taught to listen, to see, and to touch, our mother being a professional musician, and an avid collector of paintings and fine old furniture. As far back as I can remember we have all had a special rapport with the sea.

By profession I am a violinist, and by vocation a Catholic sister, a member of Our Lady's Missionaries, whose headquarters are in Toronto, Canada. It was during my novitiate in this congregation that an inherent propensity to mystical prayer was revealed and directed. It was under this community's gracious encouragement that I came to Japan in 1961 to help set up a Culture Center in Suita, near Osaka.

En route to Japan, I met a young American theologian, Michael Novak. His timely advice was that on coming to the Orient, I should have one purpose only, and that was to learn. I never forgot his words.

The first great lesson was learned during language school days, when I went to Shakado Temple on Mount Hiei overlooking Kyoto. Its solitary custodian, Somon Horisawa, opened our long friendship with the question "How do you pray?" and thus I first heard about *zazen*.

The second lesson was from that tall man among missioners, Fr. H.M. Enomiya-Lassalle S.J. "Your most valuable enrichment in Japan will be to let *zazen* teach you to pray better."

The third lesson spanned a period of four years, during which time I more or less regularly attended the Rinzai Nuns' Temple Enkoji, in Kyoto. With the guidance of Fukugai Roshi, I and the Buddhist nuns under her were taught the basics of *zazen*, and in due time were given a *koan*. Probably because of the language difficulties I misunderstood the *Sekishu Koan* (Sound of One Hand), mentally placing it in my *hara* (guts) watching and listening for its sound. However wrongly I may have interpreted the *Roshi's* teaching, I developed a strong power of concentration and one-pointedness, along with familiarity with Zen life and routine. My years at Enkoji also put me in the radius of one of the great Zen masters of the century, Shibasyama Zenkei Roshi. During *sesshin* we went daily to Nanzenji for his *teisho*.

The fourth lesson also spanned a period of about four years when, unable to withstand the rigours of Enkoji due to a rather extended bout of cancer, I continued doing *zazen* daily in our convent chapel. The visits and encouragement of the above-mentioned Buddhist monk and Catholic priest were my mainstays. One day when Horisawa San and I were doing *zazen* together, he abruptly broke the silence with, "I think it is a waste of time for you to do the *sekishu koan*. You believe Christ is within you; watch and listen to him." So, using the Zen technique, I meditated in a more Christian way, and remember reflecting some time later that this way of praying seemed to add the sense of touch, as though the breath was caressing Christ's presence.

With my return to more normal health, I accepted in August of this year [1972] Fr. Lassalle's invitation to participate in the first English retreat at Shinmeikutsu, his beautiful new *zendo* west of Tokyo. The minute I arrived, I knew it would be a good seven days. Surrounded by the familiar props of daily mass and office, I happily re-entered the Zen world with its asceticism in routine and diet and long hours of meditation. Rather soon I experienced deep and prolonged aural *makyo*.

After the retreat was over, Fr. Lassalle called me to his office. He said, "If you want *kensho* I think you can get it. I have in mind a good master for you." I answered, "I want it but . . ." and all the fears came tumbling out . . . all this probing into one's subconscious . . . fooling around with the ego...and other terms I only partially understood . . . and this by someone I didn't even know. Unperturbed, Fr. Lassalle rephrased his idea: "I'll introduce you to a *Roshi* who is a great human being, and can bring you to *kensho* easily."

And so I met Yamada Koun Roshi. He is a very comfortable man to meet, and as we proceeded through the formalities, I could not help but warm to him . . . goodness seemed to abound in him, accompanied by a very attractive openness, and a charm as natural as breathing. One by one my defences disintegrated. At one point in the conversation, his admirable wife appeared, and I was even more persuaded. The outcome was that I would become a member of the Osaka Haku-un Zazenkai, and participate in their annual *sesshin* at Takatsuki under Yamada Roshi, starting in about 10 days.

The late-August *sesshin* at Takatsuki was not a great success for me *zazen*-wise. I spent most of the time listening to the Orientation talks. It did, however, put me in step with the other members of the group, and provided the occasion to meet its selfless custodians Adachi San and Shimizu San. By the time I had completed the introductory lectures and was given formal entrance into *dokusan*, the *sesshin* was almost over, but finally, after eight years in Zen, I finally came into contact with *mu*, its first barrier the Patriarchs speak about. No thoughts, no concepts, no ideas, no theories, just pure sound in concentration . . . how delightful for a musician . . . and I was certainly enjoying the show . . . no comparison at all with the dull Rinzai *sesshins*!

In due time, I received a notification of the *Roshatsu Sesshin* to be held in Kamakura, leading up to December 8. I wrote Fr. Lassalle and invited him to join me. He replied early in November that in his 40 years of going to temples to sit, that was the first time anyone had given him any encouragement. I stuck the card in my New Testament, and because my community had made a decision to close its Japan mission, I was determined to participate. I was rested and ready. I knew it was going to be a good *sesshin*; the following is an account of what transpired, as I remember it.

First day: Just working on the sound… settled rather deeply and quickly into it…had some kind of a visual experience followed by a feeling of cleansing. At *dokusan*, the *Roshi* quickly dismissed all this…it seems I am great on the spiritual aspects… "it is the concrete you have to work on" he said as he poked my knee with his stick.

Second day: Concentration deepens…at times almost hot… sometimes one-pointedness without interruption… couldn't believe the passage of time… At *dokusan* the *Roshi* touched my knee again with his stick, asking, "What is that?" I replied… he rang the bell… I withdrew.

Third day: Deep concentration continues. *Roshi* asked, "What is *Mu*?" No idea! Perhaps one will come! Thus I entered the mysterious and centuries-old world of *Mu*. As soon as I returned to the *zendo*, decided I would have to identify with something I could check out…but used this prop only once or twice. I grabbed *mu* in a second… at least its location…firmly established within from a long way back…at 3 p.m. *dokusan*, the *Roshi* seemed pleased I had found the location, and urged me on to more depth. I tried to get beyond this location until 7 p.m. *dokusan*, but the point wouldn't budge. *Roshi* seemed puzzled by this hard core. By way of explanation I mentioned the *sekishu koan* I had worked on for years, the multiple amputations which had driven me inward, and the long practice of the Divine

Indwelling. *Roshi* raised his voice indignantly. "Don't you believe the Kingdom of God is in your little fingertip?" I looked back at him with equal indignation but could only reply without much conviction that I did.

Fourth day: Things got off to quite a different start. I was in deep concentration when I heard a cat meow outdoors. I don't know why, but something clicked ... then I checked out my new perception of an ordinary cat sound and my inner checking system was working fine ... so I listened again, and soon a dog barked but it was just a dog barking ... nothing significant there ... I told all this to the *Roshi* at the 3 o'clock *dokusan* and he smiled. "You're moving!" He asked me another impossible and senseless question ... I hesitated ... he terminated the interview. I returned to the *zendo*.

And then I started to "think," and the more I thought the more perplexed I became. I recalled the morning *teisho* (Zen talk) about Mount Fuji and Kamakura Mountain being the same height if each mountain were encompassed by the whole world. I became afraid that I would see everybody and everything in the world in the same perspective, and I felt something very basic was being challenged. I still felt alone in this *sangha* and was grateful for the presence of Fr. Lassalle. I asked permission to speak with him. He pointed out that the *Roshi* was just trying to break down my separation from things, a division that is very strong in us Westerners. I replied that I seemed to be afraid to surrender parts of my life and concepts that were very intimate and sacred to me, for an experience. I relayed the *Roshi's* challenge of the Kingdom of God in my little finger. The old priest gave his lovely slow smile, saying, "Your mental concept of and belief in the Kingdom of God in your little fingertip could be inadequate, you know. *Roshi* is trying to strengthen that faith by bringing you to the experience that this is so! Be perfectly honest and open with him. Trust him. He is a great master."

Fifth day: Deep concentration . . . gradually began to press hard until the *Roshi* noticed it and made me stop, saying it is too tiring. Gradually, by the end of the day, I grasped more and more of *mu*. A big help was during *samu* (work period) in the morning. While dusting, I ran my fingertips along the beautiful wood in the *tokanoma*, and then I saw a rather lovely wood carving. As I took it in my hands to dust, IT was so obvious that I laughed out loud. My outside world was growing by leaps and bounds . . . only the inside "me" remained encased in what seemed an impenetrable shell.

Sixth day: Tired . . . tired . . . tired . . . but in some way, relaxed and one-pointed. Today I saw the *Roshi* for the great teacher he is. Sensing my lethargy, he encouraged me by saying how close I was to getting to *kensho*, although I had no inkling of that possibility. His own energy and zeal doubled (and he was seeing 40 of us three times a day); it seemed I couldn't be budged. God's throne was in a tight, strong location. A veritable fortress.

After supper, while stretched out on the *tatami* (Japanese straw matting) during rest period, I suddenly became aware that the next day's date, the last day of the *sesshin*, was the anniversary of my entry into religious life. It would be nice if I could get *kensho* on that date. Remembering that the *Roshi* came to his experience after reading that quote of Dogen Zenji,[3] I reached for my New Testament, and it

---

[3] The words of Dogen which triggered the Roshi's great experience:
> I have come to see clearly
> That Mind is no other
> than mountains, and rivers
> and the great wide earth,
> the sun and the moon and the stars.

And a Chritian parallel which I find in John of the Cross:
> My beloved is the mountains
> And lovely wooded valleys
> Strange islands
> And resounding rivers,
> The whistling of love-stirring breezes.

opened where I had inadvertently put Fr. Lassalle's card. The first sentence that hit my eye was John's well-known phrase, "This joy, this perfect joy, is now mine." I could not help but smile. After my customary prayer to the Holy Spirit, I resumed my *zazen* . . . *dokusan* came . . . nothing clicked. *Roshi* looked at me for a while, and then asked another question about weight and *mu*. I responded, and he rang the bell for my dismissal.

On the way back to the *zendo*, I tried putting the weight into my steps . . . once at my place, I put the weight down onto the *zafu* (cushion) . . . I tucked the weight and my feet into place . . . I wriggled my body and the weight into a comfortable position . . . I slowly and consciously put the weight of my arms and hands into position . . . I looked at my controversial fingertips . . . I also remember starting to reason that they are also part of that weight and the concrete me. Then it happened. All of a sudden, the hard shell of the core center burst open, and its lovely contents poured into every pore of my entire body. It burst beyond the body boundaries, and Elaine disappeared. No boundaries anywhere. How beautiful and clean and pure . . . belonging and fitting and home-ing. How utterly perfect! My heart was bursting in gratitude.

I opened my eyes. I seemed to be in direct contact with each and every thing I saw. I looked at my fingertips. Indeed, they are filled with the Kingdom of God. I jumped up because I had to see the *Roshi*. I ran out of doors back into the *dokusan* lineup. The stars were out . . . and they were shiningly beautiful, like diamonds, and the sky a dark velvet background. They looked so friendly and reachable. I wanted to take one in to the *Roshi* in gratitude.

When I entered the *dokusan* room, the *Roshi* took one look at me and then fired all those enigmatic questions one reads about in the Zen books. It was like ABC. In utter gratitude and happiness, I could do nothing but bow my head to the *Roshi*. With infinite understanding, he touched my hair with his *kotsu* (*Roshi's* stick) and said "I confirm your *kensho*."

When I finally gained a little composure I raised my head and asked, what was that power that made the difference between one moment and the next ... what had happened? And Yamada Roshi answered as perhaps all the Zen masters and patriarchs have answered for centuries, "Call it what you will. Some say it's an intuition. Perhaps it's a light from God. In any case, you've just begun you know ... from now on you've got to become a better Christian and a better sister. So, on to the next *koan!*"

(Note: End of excerpt from "This Joy, This Perfect Joy")

A mystic's pilgrimage is not to a holy, external shrine. It is to an inner sacred place. I have found in my journey that following this method, plus a little courage and Spartan spirit and with the help of grace, we can conquer inner space. Like modern scientists learning the secrets of the universe, we can be led to enter the land of the sun, and find the light and warmth we seek so assiduously.

Chapter Ten

Pieces of a Mosaic

It is not often that we can take some small but disparate pieces of life and fit them together with a feeling of appropriateness and satisfaction. Completing a good jigsaw puzzle can sometimes come close! When I let my eye wander over a layout of a thousand pieces of a mosaic, there's a certain thrill when I see the fit in color or shape of the phenomenal world, and I can bring them together in becoming whole. This is not insignificant in my work as a teacher of meditation. Just the other day the head of a religious order reminded me that 25 years ago, as he headed for his first 30-day retreat, he heeded my advice to take along a jigsaw puzzle – and he said it saved his life!

I have seldom lived in a convent large enough to house an open table for a week's unfolding of the ultimate picture in detail of the 2,000-piece puzzle. So, more frequently, I resort to a game of solitaire where the inevitability of red on black and vice versa acts as a balm. When the spirit is ruffled, which happens from time to time, I might also spread out the cards to see what turns up. Some cards represent certain friends, and I cheer them as they appear.

Probably because according to the Enneagram, a number Seven is a head person, I prefer the games that are not all chance and leave some decision-making for the player. So I have had to invent a few of my own. One secret for a relaxing game of solitaire is that the rules must be a little flexible. By that I mean that if the game cannot be resolved by observing all the restrictions, then I can descend to level two, where one can obtain an added privilege. If I *do* resort to the age-old games that are almost impossible to resolve, I rationalize that it is preferable to create exits than be relentlessly frustrated. A bonus with all that is the fact that I am buoyed up when the Jack of Hearts or the Queen of Diamonds present themselves to keep me company.

They came to my 75th birthday party, which I want to record. I was the recipient of a unique gift from Prue Wilson, an Oxford friend and Sacred Heart sister. She gave me a day of her time, and a car in which she would chauffeur me to London for a 30-minute visit to each of four places she had chosen. As the extraordinary day unfolded, I discovered just how well she knows me.

The Queen of Diamonds
Virgins . . . Wise and Otherwise

First we drove to Roehampton, a sprawling group of convent buildings of the Religious of the Sacred Heart, which spanned centuries and has been a noted school for Catholic young girls and women. It is now an education center of true ecumenism. We had a late morning mass and a delicious lunch. It was there I discovered that Prue herself had written an autobiography of sorts, entitled *My Father Took Me to the Circus*, which tells us something about her lighthearted approach to life. She took me to the small chapel that houses the grave of Mother Janet Erskine Stewart.

Mother Stewart is my Queen of Diamonds. As I sat in the convent's old-fashioned chapel, memories of my novitiate came rushing back. The variety of hues resembled a rainbow. One of the brighter shades had to do with the novitiate rule that a novice has to make claim to a breakage if it occurs in her hands. Novices everywhere frequently break things. One day when I was a novice, there was a line-up for this declaration of culpability, and the novice in front of me clutched the frequently damaged steam iron. The sister behind me held the broken half of a toilet seat. I had a sticky pile of Christmas candy from which a pungent fragrance was emanating. My family had sent a small bottle of brandy in the midst of the hardtack – quite well disguised, but not break-proof. Note: There was not a spot of remorse among the three of us!

When I look back at novitiate now, my memory finds the colors are much more pleasant and attractive than formerly. We certainly didn't get the type of training I expected, but I gratefully experienced the unexpected. And there was a certain completeness in every day because I gradually discovered I was not in a battle, but rather on a Way that was being manifested centimeter by hard-earned centimeter. This was why I had entered. I knew I was heading for the real thing, whatever that was going to prove itself to be. At one point my friend Ernie McCullough sent a mutual friend to find out if I was happy. I sent back a "Yes!" full of smiles.

My friend Kim Wolfe Murray says learning to meditate is something like going to a spiritual boot camp. We leave the world and enter the convent with all the best will in the world, but when we sit down in silent prayer, we find we haven't left the world at all. Not just random thoughts take over, but a whole cinema of action-packed drama. Kim had gone to the Wat Pah Pong Monastery in Ubon Ratchathani, Northeast Thailand, to enter the Forest Monastery, which is run by an ancient order of monks. He had to learn to sit cross-legged on concrete floors with only a thin cotton sitting-mat for comfort and long arduous nights of meditation. And what did he find? Mosquitoes and malaria, struggles with lust, boredom, depression and even despair!

And when we taught prisoners to meditate, we quoted from Bo Lozoff's great book for detainees, *We're All Doing Time*. When they start to meditate, Bo warns the prisoners, "We may have moments of intense periods of terror, lust, perversion, fantasy, grief, guilt, greed, pride, loneliness . . . whatever furniture happens to be stored away in there, collecting cobwebs and taking up our peace." For a while, often a seemingly endless time, meditation is in a way sitting among heaven-dropped rose petals.

But in novitiate I enjoyed my meditation; it was soulmates I missed most of all, and eventually I found one in a book. That person who came closest and was able to make sense out of some of the novitiate teaching was Mother Janet Erskine Stewart. She was a woman of enormous common sense and humor, who had written copious letters to many of her charges. The day of my birthday gift, Sister Prue gave me a booklet of some of Mother Stewart's letters, and I could spot immediately the sort of help she had given me all those years ago now. One of her essays was entitled "Virgins . . . Wise and Otherwise," which is of course precisely what one discovers on entering the convent. On the other hand, she could be blunt and straightforward. Dealing with the vow of obedience, which is difficult for all religious, Mother Stewart did not hesitate for a moment to admit that the vow tended not to make us responsible people. She advocated a sort of middle course of trying to keep both passivity and action ongoing. Now, of course we are expected to be both obedient *and* responsible, which can get dodgy at times! Although I never met Mother Stewart, I feel she was one of my closest teachers.

As I sat there, I recalled the two or three times that my Novice Mistress discussed her perception that I was not in sync with the others, who were considerably younger. I certainly intended to leave if and when I got an inner message to do so, but it never came. Even as a junior professed sister, it was suggested that I leave, but the inner voice never said, "Go!" so I hung on.

In Japan, after the initial difficulties of language school, I knew I had arrived at least in the part of the world I needed most. At the end of each day as I left the Culture Centre, I exited the grounds through the church to say, "Thank you." I have done so every day since.

In 2003, it will be 50 years. I have had a wonderful life. I have enjoyed this last half century and certainly have felt fulfilled, although there have been tough times which have been bummers, as Dr. Carlson predicted. It has all been worthwhile, since suffering and the good that can accrue from it are hidden from us. The Bible says that what we have to suffer is nothing compared with what is to come. Zen would have us just BE in our pain. It is important, though, not to get sucked into our own garbage. Because I am a number Seven, my first reaction to suffering is to try to get around it or pretend it is not there. But I have learned to cope, and being the eternal optimist, find that inevitably things can only get better.

In my old age, I humbly present as representing my own, the manifesto of a prisoner who wrote, "Over the past year, I've accomplished more inside prison than I ever did outside. No drink or drugs could give me the buzz I feel when I wake up and see the sky. Rain or sunshine. There is a wonderful feeling of a private and personal linkage to something very

elemental. I feel that!" He had been helped. I feel that, too.
Sitting by Mother Stewart's grave, I realized how much help
she had given me and my heart was full of gratitude.

The King of Clubs
Bribed with Fish

At the end of my reverie in the Roehampton Chapel, I
felt a presence. There was Sister Prue with car key in hand.
Our second stop was at a Japanese grocery store. For years I
have had an interest in nutrition, and so my posting to Japan
was exactly to my taste. As my Baby Book said: "Baby can be
bribed into almost anything if fish is promised for supper." So
I was endowed with at least one helpful appetite for my first
mission assignment. I can't pretend that Japanese food went
down happily the day I arrived. In foreign travel there is a
period of adjustment when one has to become accustomed to
prevalent odors. For my first mission appointment, my
companion and I flew to Tokyo and then Kyoto, where we
were met and driven northwest to our mission hospital in
Maizuru, on the Japan Sea. I was grateful to see a baked chicken
and mashed potatoes for supper.

Now, I am devoted to Japanese food. Although one has to
be careful of the amount of salt intake, the diet is healthy and,
if chosen well, provides the minerals, vitamins, bulk and
roughage necessary for a healthy balance of body and mind.
During my six years in Oxford at the Prison Phoenix Trust,
nearly every day, I took the makings of *sushi* (a rolled rice
sandwich) in a *bento* (lunch) box, and assembled them for my
noon meal. *Sushi* restaurants are everywhere in the world now,
with a growing clientele, but unfortunately, it is expensive. It
costs much less to make it at home yourself, especially my
more relaxed variety. Good sushi is difficult to make, and also
time consuming. For recipes and instructions you can follow

at home, see the section "Making Sushi at Home" at the end of this chapter.

There are a lot of empty words written about the Japanese diet. It *is* one of the healthiest diets in the world, but only if it is eaten judiciously. Too much *tofu* too often and you imbibe too much uric acid and the joints start to ache. Too much soy sauce and *miso* and up goes the blood pressure. I know one American who had to be taken to a hospital after a five-day *sesshin*, where he was found to have very high blood pressure. Even all that meditating could not counteract the amount of salt offered in a Zen diet.

Nutritionists usually advise a variety of foods for sound health. Canadian health rules are basic and also generous, suggesting as they do three regular meals a day including breakfast. They recommend carbohydrates, vegetables, fruit, dairy products, protein and bread or cereal products to include high-fiber foods, too. The rules underline the necessity to be physically active. Recently, on a television program on healthy hearts, diet featured as a prime factor. At the end, to my delight, my cousin Bill Castelli, the cardiologist, appeared on the screen to substantiate what had gone before and point out that the amount of food for each serving is also a factor.

It was in the Orient that I learned about the body's need for water since its processes use up water in these amounts: two cups for the lungs, two for sweating, and six for intestines and kidneys. Taking into consideration the approximate four cups provided by food and metabolism, the average person needs to drink six to eight cups daily just to keep functioning.

During that day out in London with Prue, I had a nostalgic half-hour in the Japanese market. When I looked out of the shop window, there she was, waiting patiently in her little red car. I came out of the store three times with my arms loaded. Ol' Abraham would not be the only hospitable host to angels.

The Jack of Hearts
Thy sweet love remembered (Shakespeare, Sonnet 29)

Our third stop was a surprise. Hitherto I had not known of the existence of the London church of St. Clement Danes, which stands near Bush House, the home of the British Broadcasting Corporation's world service and is flanked by the Strand and Fleet Street. The church is dedicated to Royal Air Force (RAF) personnel who lost their lives on duty. I looked around and then sat down, slowly flicking through the pages of my mind and the hundreds of RAF men the MacInnes family had entertained at our home in New Brunswick during the Second World War.

In the middle of London I was, in a sense, once again opening that front door of our Botsford Street home in Moncton to three RAF men on a cold and blustery Canadian February evening in 1942. Two of them I knew. As they reached down to brush the snow off their boots, my glance rose to meet another pair of eyes holding mine. Time stood still for a split second. I remembered feeling held, realizing this wasn't a stare but rather a discovery. Some people say it can happen like that. Chemistry changes in a moment. I was only 17 at the time, but able to hold his eyes, because there was something different there which I found attractive.

His name was Jack. He kept popping up at my side all that evening as my sisters and I served food and music to our guests. I remember lots of good conversation, good food and good music. The next night we went out together – and the next and the next . . . to a dance or a flick (movie) or tobogganing or skating.

Over the following weeks, I became more and more aware that someone from far away was invading my life in a loving and inclusive way. A new, inner area which had something to do with the heart was expanding. A door was opening, and I was conscious of a brewing inner change, something that made me cautious, yet at the same time grateful for the presence of my parents and sisters.

I was happy in my bewilderment. Still, I have a distinct memory of recalling an insight while standing in the downstairs hall of our home, between the front door and living room. This was the sure knowledge that to love and be loved in return is music and poetry and art all rolled into one great unfathomable wonder. I can see yet the very spot in our home where I experienced that warming thought, and perhaps also the wide innocent grin which probably accompanied it.

Jack, a farmer who loved the earth, went on to Florida to learn to fly. After getting his Wings he returned to Moncton. I was at Mount Allison University in nearby Sackville and had arranged for him to stay at the Marshlands, a charming inn in Sackville. I even asked to see the room where he would be staying, and it was truly lovely, I thought, with an English countryside atmosphere (although at the time I had never seen the English countryside!). It was October, the loveliest of months in Maritime Canada. Jack had never seen such riotous colors as a Canadian autumn provides so lavishly. We were strangely silent that afternoon as we kicked up the fallen leaves walking through the woods for tea at Frosty Hollow. That evening there was a campus dance, and I recall with chagrin that I wouldn't dance with anyone else but Jack.

After several weeks in the Maritimes, all too soon he had to leave. He was to fly a bomber home to England the next day. That last evening together, the war became "the damn war," as we desperately planned for the uncertain time when peace might come. Jack was a farmer, and he spoke lovingly of Cammeringham, the house and farm given to him by his father. He described market day at home and how cute little pigs really are. He was a real man of the earth. His heart and plans were as one, growing and leaping ahead, and I remember how eager and sure and decided he was. Although I knew I would love farming, I was also a bundle of awakening womanhood, unsure of many things, including England. He promised to come back to Canada for me after the war, to show me England and Cammeringham. And so he left 187 Botsford Street, just as he had arrived about a year earlier on a cold and blustery night.

The following August, returning home from a shopping trip, I was in the same insight-laden spot in our downstairs hall when I saw a telegram addressed to me. Jack had been killed in Devon while returning from operations. Interment was to be at his family's home in Scampton. The music changed to a minor key, and the poetry and art spoke of shadow and death. I was 19 and Jack was dead at 23. Even now, he remains always young and enthusiastic and optimistic, and it is I who am the hostage of time.

Fifty years to the day later, Jack's brother and sister and I gathered at Scampton and remembered him with prayer and music and poetry. I chose to read some of the words of Rupert Brooke, who spoke so eloquently of those who died in the First World War, to which I had added a few pertinent additions.

> His heart was woven of human joys and cares
> Washed marvellously with sorrow, swift to mirth,
> Those few years had given him gentleness; dawn was his
> And sunset, and that feeling of the earth.
>
> He had seen movement, and heard music,
> Known slumber and waking; loved; gone proudly be-
> friended,
> Felt the quick stir of wonder; rode,
> Touched flowers and mane and lips.
>
> Now we see him in waters blown by changing winds to
> laughter,

And lit by the rich skies of England, all day.
And after frost, with a gesture,
He stays the waves that dance
In a wandering loveliness.

He leaves a white unbroken glory
A gathered silence
A width of shining peace.

In a way, my Jack of Hearts *was* to show me England and the lovely Cammeringham Manor. Since I first came to England, it has been my home away from home. The present incumbent is Jack's nephew and namesake (known as "John") and is master there. His heart and home are big enough to include an aging nun. He is joint-master of the local hunt, very smart in his brilliant riding gear, and his wife and children share his love of horses. I happily wander for hours through the old house and farm and fields and barns, often with his young son James in tow.

Cammeringham Manor dates back to a foundation of white-robed monks and was built around 1250. It now has a Queen Anne front and Jacobean rear, although part of the old monastery moat still exists. The family has maintained the remains of the chapel with utmost perfection. The house is built of local yellow stone, with the ancient quarry right on the property. There is a multitude of barns, and thousands of acres of grain. John began his stewardship by planting 20,000 trees, three small forests, in his children's names. He received the country's top award for his efforts in rural conservation. Numerous country trails and paths lead to the lovely retirement home of Jack's brother and sister-in-law. One can wander on foot, by bicycle, horse, or car mile after picturesque mile.

That extraordinary day in London in 2000, despite the fact that a visit to the RAF Memorial was supposed to be quiet and reflective, I suddenly burst out laughing. I remember

Jack trying to sell me the idea of being a farmer, by earnestly relating how charming baby pigs can be. And that day in London, I thought of my four years on the island of Leyte in the Philippines where I endeavored to help the locals replace their ailing pig population there. When our prime sow was giving birth to her first litter, those involved in the project were standing around watching Undoy, the man who owned the farm, deal with each newborn. Eight little piglets came forth in quick succession. There was a considerable pause towards the end, and then suddenly, the *ihid* (runt) of the litter came flying out in mid-air, to the great delight of us all, with each of us trying to catch the slippery little parcel as it sailed along. I felt I heard Jack laugh, too.

Jack's body lies not at Cammeringham but in the family plot at Scampton churchyard, about 5 kilometers south. It is a lovely English country churchyard. The family gave some of their adjoining property for RAF graves of other airmen who were killed in the area, including several Germans shot down nearby. It is a place of utmost peace and tranquillity. From Scampton House, where Jack and his brother and sister were brought up, we can see the cross on his grave, which turns to gold in the setting sun. My 30 minutes in the London chapel passed quickly, and I wrote his name in the book of remembrance. My Jack of Hearts has been a great blessing in my life. His destiny was to be young at that dark time.

Ace of Spades
Illumined with Fluid Gold

The fourth and final stop that day was at the Tate Art Gallery. That wasn't a surprise, but the answer to a long-held wish. About five years before, I had been sent a message on a postcard bought at the gallery which featured a copy of the Turner masterpiece *Norham Castle*. Even on a small, postcard-sized reproduction, I was captivated, but it was months before I discovered the reason. I knew it was connected with something I had been pondering for years: Would I ever discover a painting that I would identify as being mystical? In one sense, all great art represents IT.

Turner painted Norham Castle five times, each time more simply than the one before. My choice was the last, painted not long before he died: a celebration of sunrise. It is almost simply "sunlight." Perhaps it was the emptiness of form that attracted me.

Generally speaking, Zen art tends to be cryptic. *Koans* are cryptic: "Does the dog have Buddha Nature or not?" "*Mu!*"

A *haiku* is a cryptic verse of 17 syllables. Basho is the master of *haiku*, and his most famous verse is about a frog sitting beside an old pond. A cryptic translation would be:

Frog
old pond
plop!

That says it all. But as my editor keeps reminding me, sometimes this is not quite enough for a Westerner. I have read many attempts at translating this *haiku* which most often turns out something like:

A frog
Sitting on the edge of an old pond
Jumps into the water and makes a splash.

Oh, my! How labored! How apt to Zen, the cryptic version. I feel invited into the empty spaces that Basho has created. That is where I find mysticism. In the empty spaces. I have often wondered how an artist would paint empty spaces. What would a painting of the Buddha Nature look like? IT cannot be seen, IT cannot be heard, IT cannot be felt, IT cannot be tasted. How can anyone paint that! In our terms, it would have to be empty. Then one day this Turner postcard arrived. I did not make that connection at first, and simply put the reproduction on the mantel of the fireplace. I kept looking at it. I had been told the original hung in the Tate. I promised myself to go there one day to see it. Prue remembered, and her little red car took me to the front steps.

I found *Norham Castle* in the best possible position. Large. Glowing. Alive. Life-ing. Light-ing. There IT was in all glory. God alive and manifesting. Turner painted IT as "light," the dissolving power of light. I remembered as I stood there drinking IT in, that Yamada Roshi had bestowed on me the Zen name of "Light." That day at the Tate, I saw a radiant representation of inner LIFE at sunrise, with one animal toward the foreground, just distinct enough to be recognized, bending to drink. All else is indistinct, unformed and unforgettable, "illumined with fluid gold." It is not cryptic. It is less than that. IT IS. I just stood still for 25 minutes, cutting down the separation to connection. I understand from what I have read that the painting is unfinished. Which accounts for my fascination. I was not inactive while I stood there gazing. IT was be-ing completed. Connecting and reciprocating!

I ran down to the bookstore in my last allotted five minutes and found a large copy of the painting, which I brought back to my flat and later had framed. It hangs where there is both natural light by day and an artificial light for nightfall. IT is right before my eyes whenever I return home, and connects immediately. It turned my flat into a hermitage. I had always thought a hermit lived alone, but not so! Being a hermit is living with the life-ing potential which fills creation. It is be-ing. I didn't find it. It found me when I was ready. I am grateful.

Finale

Turner's later paintings, much of Brahms, some French music, and Rilke's poetry all are ready friends and points of connection and reciprocity. I live now not I, but Christ lives within me. That Christian promise came to life in me through Buddhist hands. Sometimes I sit by the sea with a litany, and the response to each memory is "thank you." People, places, events, past, present, are all a now, here, and forever.

They could fit in 17 syllables very easily. For my own benefit, I chant them through. The Celtic ancestors live on in our family. And the future is full of promise. I have a date in 2004 to go to Morvern in the western Highlands right across from the Isle of Mull and raise the fiddle once again where Clan MacInnes set sail for Canada many years ago. Nephew Michael MacInnes is rebuilding the Fiddler's Cottage there, and we will assemble and tell the tales of our journeys. Another circle is completed; this one took 168 years. Strathspeys will be danced and poetry recited and the longing momentarily assuaged.

Homecoming is doubtless just offshore, the final One-ing. The senses which opened the door to experience are gradually closing, and a complete mystical treatise should deal with each of them. But the eye and the ear are closest to the heart, and as Yamada Roshi used to say, the secret in meditation is not to stop there.

And so when I returned to Canada and went for my millennium stroll along the New Brunswick beach, I took all of those 75 years with me and savored them one by one. I was born by the sea and into a musical family with the Celtic longing in my heart. As the sound of the Atlantic Ocean waves broke into my reverie, I recalled that the joy of the raindrop is to enter the ocean. Sometimes I see IT as something very special, and want to use capital letters. But gradually "it" is becoming an everyday affair, which is nothing special at all. As I teach this both inside and outside of prisons, I find I am not dabbling in an esoteric mysticism; I am merely selling water by the river.

Making Sushi at Home

Start the homemade variety by going to an Oriental store and buying the following ingredients:

- Japanese rice (glutinous)
- *takuan* (a long, pickled radish)
- a tube of *wasabi* (hot green horseradish)
- a bottle of Kikkoman soy sauce
- a packet of *nori* (a marine algae, seaweed)
- a *sudare* (a bamboo mat for rolling which is helpful and cheap)

The two varieties we are considering are *maki sushi* (rolled sushi) and *negiri sushi* (ball sushi). If you don't have a rice cooker, use 2-1/4 cups of rice to 2-1/2 cups of water. Leave the rice uncovered until it boils vigorously for 1 minute, then lower the heat, cover, and cook for 18 minutes, leaving the lid on at all times. After 18 minutes, allow the rice to sit away from the heat for at least 15 minutes. Uncover, and turn out in a large, open dish, and sprinkle with a mixture of 1/2 cup of sugar, 1/2 cup of rice vinegar, and 2-1/2 cups of water. Fluff the rice with 2 paddles or dampened wooden mixing spoons. This rice mixture can be used with either *maki sushi* (rolled) or the *negiri* (small rice-rectangles that are topped with fish). When the rice mixture is room temperature, it can be covered until used.

In making these two traditional varieties, great care must be taken to have only the best quality, especially for fish, meat, vegetables, pickle (said to enhance digestion) and *nori* (seaweed), which is shiny and greenish and contains lots of iron. Insist on Japanese quality ingredients. They are in short supply even in Japan. Substitutes are anathema. The vegetable and protein ingredients can be purchased from a Western grocer. For rolled *sushi,* a beginner could choose four or five of the easy-to-use

215

ingredients, such as: smoked salmon, cooked ham (not delicatessen), cooked or canned asparagus tips, cooked baby green beans, a stick cut from the long pickle, and a thin cooked carrot.

To roll the *maki sushi,* place one large sheet of *nori* (seaweed) on the *sudare* (bamboo mat) and, with slightly wet hands, spread about 1/4 cup of the prepared rice on the seaweed, leaving a bit of an edge at the top. Lay whatever you choose, one of protein, two or three vegetables, and pickle, width-wise on the rice, keeping them as close together as possible. The top edge of the *nori* is then moistened slightly. Beginning with the lower edge, using the bamboo roller to compress the mixture as a sandwich, and with a great deal of help from your fingers, roll it up and press the moistened edge of the *nori.* Either bite into it immediately while the seaweed is crisp or allow this to stand for a few minutes. With a very sharp dampened knife, cut the roll of *sushi* in slices about 2 cm wide. It should be eaten immediately or the *nori* will become damp and tough.

For a small party, I find it easiest to allow the guests to make their own, in which case, I cut the large sheet of nori into two smaller rectangular sheets. Then one can pile on the desired ingredients and the nori remains crisp and easy to bite. All the above-mentioned ingredients are arranged in buffet style. The guests can decide themselves what they want and assemble the *sushi.* It may not look as perfect as a Japanese restaurant serving, but the taste should be top class.

The *negiri sushi* is assembled using the above rice mixture, brushed with a swab of wasabi, and topped with a piece of raw fish or egg omelette. Voilà! There is your *sushi.* Raw fish must always be extremely fresh. Japan is a country of four islands and so fresh raw fish is available every day. This delicacy is called *sashimi* (sah-she-mee). It must not be frozen. Keep inquiring until you find the right fishmonger, and she or he will proudly carve you the required amount in the traditional way. In the battle with expanding waistlines, *sashimi* is often served separately. Raw tuna is an international favorite, but in Canada, it runs second to raw Atlantic salmon, which is superlative. Shrimp, raw or cooked, is also popular, and so is a piece of cooked lobster. Delicious! Tai (pinkish white fish) is another favorite for an educated palate, and has a rather subtle taste. I hesitate to recommend other fish for a beginner, because many varieties tend to have a strong and fishy flavor, but the Japanese love *ika (*squid) and *tako (*octopus), mostly because they have to be chewed well.

When eating *sushi,* it is advised to lubricate the digestive tract with hot *sake* (rice wine). Like grape wine, it has different varieties. *Ikkyu* (top class) is worthy of the best sushi, and is heated in a *tokkuri* (an 8-cm container), usually in a pan of hot water, then poured into your own *choko* (little drinking cup), which holds one mouthful. *Sake* is never diluted, and is served hot. In Japan your eating companion will keep your little cup full from the *sake* in your own *tokkuri.*

The condiments served with *sushi* are also important. Just about everyone is familiar with *wasabi,* a strong, greenish mustard, but I understand it is really Japanese horseradish. It seems to be unrelated to horseradish, but we come to remember it as the tearfully pungent green paste that accompanies *sushi.* The very best *wasabi* is the grated root which has a compelling herbal fragrance, and in its powdered form is the most expensive and difficult to find. It is best known here in Canada in tube form (which one book says has nothing going for it except convenience). However, there is another impersonator on stage in Toronto restaurants these days, where we are often served *wasabi* in a ball shape. Whatever its source, it not only lacks the traditional bite and taste, but it also does not disintegrate well with the soy sauce. So I vote for *wasabi* in a tube.

Next, the important soy sauce. Old Japan hands will not tolerate any substitute for Kikkoman. Their advertisements in Japan say it all: "Don't ask for soy sauce, just say Kikkoman." It is a must for Japanese food. There is a "lite" variety now for those watching their salt intake and neither version contains any of the dreaded monosodium glutamate. As a dip, put about 2 tbsp of Kikkoman and a squirt of *wasabi* in a small saucer, and mix together until they are fully blended.

For the egg mixture, heat 1 tsp oil in frying pan, and mix 1 large beaten egg with 1 tsp water. Pour over the pan to cover base. Lift the edges to allow extra liquid to flow underneath, until the omelette is nearly done. Remove from the pan and allow it to set and cool. Roll up and cut into 1- to 2-cm strips. One strip of this can replace the raw fish in an open *sashimi* (raw fish) serving.

After the *sake*, you switch to green tea. It complements whatever you are eating and puts all in the contents of the stomach to rest. At this point in my life, I am fussier about green tea than almost any other Japanese food. But coming to relish the fine points of green tea is like coming to *satori*, you KNOW, but only for yourself. Only *you* can discover what your favorite is. Good green tea is expensive and is supposed to be green when you drink it. If it is brown in color, it is either second class (and has a dusty taste), or it is old. By the way, treat yourself to a Japanese teacup as well.

Dessert is a bowl of varied fruit, peeled and cut in small chunks, and served with a toothpick. A dry, slightly sweet cookie can be served to accompany the fruit, and comes in many varieties. They usually are very attractive. No squishy cakes allowed, and in the summer, mouthfuls of chilled melon and cold *mugi-cha* (wheat tea) are great refreshers.

A word about *tofu* (bean curd) which is another Oriental delicacy that deserves a mention. Beginners find it tasteless, but a good Oriental cook makes it sing, and it is an excellent source of protein. In my day, Kamakura was said to have the best *tofuya-san* (*tofu* maker) in Japan, who rose at 2:00 a.m. each day to start a new batch so that it was freshly made every day. The little store was near the house I lived in, and it was a treat to buy a small slab of the silk variety, and transform its taste by simply serving it with a sauce of a medium *miso* (fermented bean curd) and a little sugar. Mostly we used *tofu* in soups. The Japanese tend to use clear soup, flavored with *miso* (mee-soh), which comes in a variety of fermentation. The dark *miso* is very strong and preferred by traditionalists (especially in *zendos*), but lighter varieties are the most appropriate for non-Japanese beginners. As salt is used in the fermentation, care must be taken in using *miso* judiciously.

For extra flavor use *shitake* mushrooms in Japanese cooking. Soak them in hot water for 30 minutes. Cut off the hard stalk, cut them into thin strips and cook them gently in 2 tbsp Kikkoman and 1 tbsp water for five minutes. You can sneak them into *sushi*, or soup, or any food that is complemented by an addition of mushrooms.

Glossary of Japanese
and Sanskrit Words Used

ango: period of quiet retreat; usually 100 days duration, twice annually

aikido: art of self-defense by meeting the spirit of the other

chonan: eldest son in a Japanese family

Denkoroku: Rinzai book of 54 *koans*

dhyana: (Sanskrit) meditation. Channa/Chan in Chinese. Zenna/Zen in Japanese.

dojo: place of practice

dokusan: private interview, where disciple's state of insight is tested

gassho: gesture of raising the hands, palm to palm before the face, to indicate respect, gratitude or humility or all three

gedo: outside-the-way Zen

Hekiganroku: Bluecliff Record *Rinzai* book of 100 *koans*

hibachi: deep brazier

Hinayana: the small-vehicle Buddhism

ikebana: flower arrangement; literally, "living flowers"

joriki: settling power

judo: art of self-defense

kado: art of flower arrangement

kaikan: auditorium

kendo: art of fencing

kensho godo: the Way of enlightenment

kinhin: walking meditation

koan: a conundrum which the intellect cannot solve

kokoro: the heart-mind/mind-soul

koto: Japanese floor harp

kyosaku: stick for massaging back and shoulder muscles

Kyosho: Sanbo Kyodan bi-monthly magazine

kyudo: the art of archery

Mahayana: the large-vehicle Buddhism

maki sushi: rice and vegetables and protein rolled in seaweed

makyo: surfacing of inner residue on the surface of the mind

michi: the Way; Japanese translation of Chinese *do*

mondo: questions and answers, Zen repartee

Mumonkan: perhaps the most famous collection of (48) *koans*

mudra: hand position during practice

nori: a marine algae, or seaweed, a wrapper for *maki sushi*

rohatsu: Zen retreat prior to December 8

rosan: 12-year period of severe discipline in *Tendai* Buddhism

Roshi: honorary title, sometimes given to a Zen master; lit. "Old teacher"

sado: the art of tea

saijojo: Zen of the highest vehicle in Buddhism

sakura: cherry blossom

samadhi: (Sanskrit) deeper than the ordinary state of consciousness

sangha: community of disciples

satori: enlightenment

sashimi: raw fish

sesshin: Zen retreat; literally, "encounter of the heart"

Shakado:Tendai temple on Mount Hiei

shikantaza: just sitting

Shinmeikutsu: Jesuit *zendo* west of Tokyo

shodo: art of Calligraphy

shoken: first interview with teacher

Shoyoroku: Book of Serenity: a *Soto* book of 100 *koans*

sushi: cold rice garnished with raw fish or vegetables

Tathagata: pure coming and going; absolute appearance

teisho: a Zen talk

Theravada: Way of the Elders

wasan: Hakuin Zenji's *Song of Zazen*

zabuton: large, flat cushion for sitting

zafu: round, high cushion for sitting, placed in the center of the *zabuton*

zammai: deeper than ordinary state of consciousness

zazen: sitting meditation

Books Consulted

Armstrong, Karen. *A History of God*. New York: Ballantine Books, 1993.

——. *Buddha*. Great Britain: Weidenfield and Nicolson, 2000.

Aitken, Robert. *A Zen Wave*. Weatherhill, 1978.

——. *Taking the Path of Zen*. San Francisco: North Point Press, 1982.

——. *The Mind of Clover*. San Francisco: North Point Press, 1984.

Bancroft, Anne. *Women in Search of the Sacred*. Arkana/Penguin, 1996.

Batchelor, Stephen. *The Awakening of the West*. Aquarian, 1994.

Bertell, Rosalie. *Planet Earth*. London: The Women's Press Limited, 2000.

Brueggemann, Walter. *Hopeful Imagination*. United States of America: Fortress Press, 1986.

Castelli, William P. and Glen C. Griffin. *Good Fat, Bad Fat: Lower Your Cholesterol and Reduce Your Odds of a Heart Attack*. Tucson: Fisher Books, 2000.

Cleary, Thomas. *No Barrier*. Aquarian/Thorsons, 1993.

Collins, Kenneth. *Exploring Christian Spirituality*. Grand Rapids, MI: Baker Books, 2000.

Dalglish, Jack. *Eight Metaphysical Poets*. Heinemann, 1961.

de Gasztold, Carmen. *Prayers from the Ark*. Toronto: MacMillan, 1967.

de Mello, Anthony. *Contact with God*. Gujarat Sahitya Prakash, India, 1990.

de Waal, Esther. *The Celtic Way of Prayer.* London: Hodder & Stoughton, 1996.

Enomiya-Lassalle, Hugo. *Living in the New Consciousness.* Shambhala, 1988.

———. *The Practice of Zen Meditation.* London: Aquarian Press, 1992.

Flemming, Ursula (ed). *Meister Eckhart: The Man from Whom God Hid Nothing.* Herefordshire: Gracewing, 1995.

Foster, Nelson and Jack Shoemaker. *A New Zen Reader.* The Ecco Press, 1996.

Fox, Matthew. *Meditations with Meister Eckhart.* Santa Fe, NM: Bear and Company, Inc., 1983.

Graham, Dom Aelred. *Zen Catholicism.* New York: Crossroad, 1994.

Herrigel, Eugen. *Zen and the Art of Archery.* Arkana Penguin, 1985.

Hill, David. *Turner in the North.* New Haven: Yale University Press, 1996.

Johnston, William. *Arise, My Love...* Maryknoll, NY: Orbis, 2000.

Kabat-Zinn, Jon. *Full Catastrophe Living.* Piatkus, 1990.

Kapleau, Philip. *The Three Pillars of Zen.* New York: Doubleday, 1989.

Kelsey, Morton. *The Other Side of Silence.* Mahwah, NJ: Paulist Press, 1995.

Larisey, Peter. *Light for a Cold Land.* Hamilton, ON: Dundurn Press, 1973.

Lewis, C. S. *A Grief Observed.* London: Faber and Faber, 1961.

Lozoff, Bo. *We're All Doing Time.* Durham, NC: Human Kindness Foundation, 1992.

MacInnes, Elaine. *Light Sitting in Light.* Philippines: Zen Center for Oriental Spirituality in the Philippines, 1999.

———. *Zen and the Art of Spiritual Maintenance.* Canada, 2000.

MacInnes, Elaine and Chubb. *Becoming Free Through Meditation and Yoga.* Oxford: Prison Phoenix Trust, 1995.

MacLeod, Alistair. *No Great Mischief.* Toronto: McClelland & Stewart, 2001.

Maguire, Jack. *Waking Up.* Woodstock, VT: Skylight Paths Publishing, 2000.

McPherson, Anne. *Walking to the Saints: A Little Pilgrimage Through France.* Ottawa: Novalis, 2000.

Millar, Henry. *The Smile at the Foot of the Ladder.* ND Paperback NDP 386 USA.

Mommaers, Paul and Jan Van Bragt. *Mysticism: Buddhist and Christian.* New York: Crossroad, 1995.

Monahan, Maud. *Life and Letters of Janet Erskine Stewart.* London: Longmans, Green and Co., 1923.

Nakamura Hajime. *Gottama Buddha.* Kyoto: Buddhist Books International, 1958.

Newell, J. Philip. *Celtic Benediction: Morning and Evening Prayer.* Ottawa: Novalis, 2000.

Nhat Hanh, Thich. *Peace Is Every Step.* New York: Bantam, 1991.

———. *Living Buddha, Living Christ.* Riverhead Books, 1995.

O'Donohue, John. *Anam Cara.* New York: Cliff Street Books/ Harper Collins, 1997.

O'Murchu, Diarmuid, msc. *Our World in Transition.* Sussex, England: The Book Guild Limited, 1995.

———. *A Radical Option for Life.* New York: Crossroad, 1999.

——. *Religion in Exile.* New York: Crossroad, 2000.

Rahner, Karl. *The Three Jewels: Root Source.* Manila: Zendo, 1986.

Rilke, Rainer Maria. *Poems from the Book of Hours.* New York: New Directions Book, 1975.

——. *Love Poems to God.* Riverhead Books, 1996.

——. *Diaries of A Young Poet.* New York: W.W. Norton & Company, 1998.

Riso, Don Richard and Russ Hudson. *The Wisdom of the Enneagram.* New York: Bantam Books, 1999.

Sato and Kuzunishi. *The Zen Life.* Weatherhill/Tankosha, 1987.

Schumacher, E.F. *A Guide for the Perplexed.* New York: Harper & Row, 1997.

Shorres, Eric, *Turner the Great Watercolours.* London: Royal Academy of Arts, 2001.

Smiles, Sem. *J.M.W. Turner.* London: Tate Gallery Publishing Limited, 2000.

Stewart, Janet E. *Essays and Papers.* Roehampton, 1915.

——. *Highways and By-ways in the Spiritual Life.* London: Longmans, Green and Co., 1923.

Suzuki, David. *The Sacred Balance.* British Columbia: Graystone Books, The Mountaineers, David Suzuki Foundation, 1997.

Suzuki, Shinichi. *Zen Mind, Beginners Mind.* Weatherhill, 1970.

Swick, David. *Thunder and Ocean: Shambala and Buddhism in Nova Scotia.* Lawrencetown, NS: Pottersfield Press, 1996.

Wolfe Murray, Kim. "Theravada Buddhist Monasticism in the West: A Personal View" in *Thomas Merton Review,* England, January 2001.

Yamada, Koun. *Gateless Gate.* Tucson: The University of Arizona Press, 1990.

About the Author

Born in 1924 in Moncton, New Brunswick, in Atlantic Canada, Elaine MacInnes attended university at nearby Mount Allison Conservatory of Music, where she studied violin, then moved to New York City where she studied at Juilliard School of Music. She taught music at Mount Royal College Conservatory in Calgary, Alberta, and played in the Calgary and Edmonton symphony orchestras.

She left Calgary in 1953 and entered Our Lady's Missionaries, a Canadian foreign mission community. Her first overseas assignment was to Japan in 1961. While helping to found a culture center, she became interested in Buddhism and was soon introduced to its meditation, *zazen*. She studied with Rinzai Buddhist nuns at Enkoji in Kyoto, and after eight years joined the Soto Zen Sanbo Kyodan at Kamakura under Yamada Koun Roshi, who eventually invited her to proceed to their program of *koan* studies.

After 15 years in Japan, Sister Elaine transferred to the Philippines in 1976 and shortly afterward was invited to open a Zen Center for the Catholic Church in Manila. While pursuing her apostolate in animal husbandry among the poor, she was fired by interest in helping Filipino Christians develop an Asian spirituality. In 1980, Yamada Roshi invested both Sister Elaine and Father H.M. Enomiya-Lassalle S.J. as *Roshi*. They were the first Roman Catholics to receive this accreditation, which is spiritual transmission. In Manila, she taught Zen for four years to political detainees who had been tortured while incarcerated duing the worst of the Marcos years. The therapeutic effects of sitting in silent meditation became eminently evident. Sister Elaine saw the detainees change from an angry, tense, enervated and incapacitated group of individuals to a relaxed, sociable, energized and effective team. This experience led her to become an enthusiastic believer in

Restorative Justice and the idea that prisons should be not punitive, but rather places of hope and healing.

In February 1993, the current head of the Sanbo Kyodan, Kubota Jiun Roshi, went to the Philippines. Upon recognizing the three Filipino teachers trained by Sister Elaine, he officially turned the Zen Center Philippines over to Filipino teachers. In 2001 the Center celebrated its 25th anniversary.

Sister Elaine was, in 1992, free to accept the invitation of Ann Wetherall to become Director of the Prison Phoenix Trust, Oxford, which encourages prisoners in the United Kingdom to use their cell as a place of spiritual practice with the Oriental disciplines of meditation and yoga. From her own experience, Sister Elaine felt that the best way forward was to train teachers to teach in their local prisons. Her Trust maintained contact by letter with more than 2000 inmates concerning their efforts in silent meditation. By the time of her retirement in 1999, the Trust had placed teachers in 86 prisons throughout the UK and Eire. Some wittily call it "Zen and the Art of Doing Time."

In May 1996, HarperCollins published Sister Elaine's fourth book, *Light Sitting in Light*. In May 1998, she was awarded an honorary degree, Doctor of Laws, from her alma mater, Mount Allison University, in New Brunswick. On February 14, 2001, her Excellency the Right Honourable Adrienne Clarkson, Governor General of Canada, named Sister Elaine as an Officer of the Order of Canada, which honors Canadians for exemplary achievement, with the following citation:

> She offers those who are incarcerated a path to hope and peace. Sister Elaine founded and ran a conservatory-style cultural centre near Osaka, Japan. As she introduced Western music to the region, she was introduced to Zen. Later becoming one of the world's few Zen Masters, she taught meditation to prisoners in the Philippines and Great Britain, helping to improve their concentration, sociability and

self-esteem. Her approach flourished, with thousands of inmates benefiting from her persistence and compassion. She has returned to Canada and is now initiating similar programs here.

In, 2002, Sister Elaine was awarded the Commemorative Medal from Queen Elizabeth II for making a profound and lasting contribution to British society.

Sister Elaine MacInnes's Zen Name

Ko-un-ang

Hermitage of the Cloud of Light

Teachers in the Anbo Kyodan lineage are usually given names ending in "cloud" – *un* in Japanese – with only the prefix being distinctive. The virtual founder of the lineage was Harada Dai-un, which means "Large Cloud." His successor was Yasutani Haku-un, which means "White Cloud." The third in line was Yamada Ko-un, "Ploughing Cloud," the teacher of Sister Elaine. She was also given the same sounding name, Ko-un, but the kanji for *ko* is "light." The *ang* is a feminine suffix which literally means "hermitage."

Perhaps Sister Elaine was given this name because her teacher said that for the Christian, the concretized Essential Nature is often expressed as "light." The ancient Sanskrit for the kanji had the original meaning of "keeper of the holy flame."

The following are three computer-generated transcriptions of the three kanji, which are read from top to bottom: